Other Books by Genie Craff:

PIP$ PROFIT$ & POWER FOREX MINDSET MASTERY JOURNAL
Hold My Hand: Remedy for my Destiny
Stallin' Callin' Money Making Phone Calls – Working from Home
Lost CHAPTERS: Think & Grow Rich
Coming Soon:
YOUR Affection Connection: Love and Sensual Memory
Finally, It's ALL About Me! Personal BRANDING

PIP$ PROFIT$ & POWER

FOREX MINDSET MASTERY

GENIE CRAFF

authorHOUSE

AuthorHouse™
1663 Liberty Drive
Bloomington, IN 47403
www.authorhouse.com
Phone: 1 (800) 839-8640

© 2020 Genie Craff. All rights reserved.

No part of this book may be reproduced, stored in a retrieval system, or transmitted by any means without the written permission of the author.

Published by AuthorHouse 02/06/2020

ISBN: 978-1-7283-4351-8 (sc)

Library of Congress Control Number: 2019920670

Printed in the United States of America.

Any people depicted in stock imagery provided by Getty Images are models, and such images are being used for illustrative purposes only.
Certain stock imagery © Getty Images.

This book is printed on acid-free paper.

Because of the dynamic nature of the Internet, any web addresses or links contained in this book may have changed since publication and may no longer be valid. The views expressed in this work are solely those of the author and do not necessarily reflect the views of the publisher, and the publisher hereby disclaims any responsibility for them.

CONTENTS

Dedication vii
Acknowledgements / Reviews...ix
Forex Mindset Mastery Introduction xi

Chapter 1: Mindset Mastery, Belief & Confidence Building 1
Chapter 2: Focus On Why.. 18
Chapter 3: Consistent Confidence & Mentoring......................................28
Chapter 4: Prosperity Trading Plan 52
Chapter 5: Unbreakable Trading Rules 64
Chapter 6: Trade Entry And Exit Indicators... 75
Chapter 7: Forex Education ~ Incorporating Daily Learning................. 83
Chapter 8: Passion And Greed 91
Chapter 9: Responsible Risk Management 105
Chapter 10: Women In Forex (For Your Eyes Only)............................... 114
Chapter 11: Vision, Success, And Big Dream 126
Chapter 12: Abundant Gratitude Lifestyle 146
Chapter 13: Challenge Completion Log... 154

Conclusion 159

"Honesty is the first chapter in the book of wisdom."
~~Thomas Jefferson

DEDICATION

*""It's possible", said Pride. "It's Risky," said Experience.
"It's pointless", said Reason. "Give it a try", whispered the Heart." ~~Anonymous*

This work is dedicated to all FOREX traders who desire MINDSET MASTERY. Traders prepare their minds for consistently profitable trades with enduring focus, planned trading and regular journaling. With full confidence, FOREX traders incorporate daily knowledge and wisdom for a prosperous lifestyle of Abundant Gratitude.

"I Made Money"
"I made money!! Carly age 10 announced, ever so proudly... (I thought she was going to show me her first corporate paycheck!) "Well, it is a whole lot of green...." My voice trailed off as I examined the full spectrum of "the giant 8" X 22" hand-colored greenback I held in my hands. "Tell me about your money!" I said, noting this was indeed the most unusual "dollar bill" I'd ever seen.

"It's lots of money on one paper! It is a $26 dollar bill!"

"A $26 dollar bill?" I questioned. "Yes! It is the best idea ever!! Now people won't have to have lots of those little dollars. They can have all their dollars in one big dollar!" she continued. I guess that is kind of a good idea, I smiled silently to myself, thinking about adults who would agree with her. "I am going to keep it and take it to the bank.

That is where you keep your money.", she stated.

~~Genie Craff

HOLD MY HAND Remedy for My Destiny p. 150, (Abridged)

ACKNOWLEDGEMENTS / REVIEWS

"Phenomenal! Can't wait to read the whole book!" ~ L. D., Oakland Park, FL

"This is AWESOME! Mindset is what will keep traders trading for the long term. This professional journal makes people think. It could make them come back for more knowledge. ~ M. S. Parkland, FL

"I love all the great information. I believe this will be a very helpful tool for many traders just starting out. Patience is the key to successful trading." ~ K. S., Tampa, FL

"I LOVE the quotes! They provide a tiny bit of motivation at just the right time." ~ M. R. Las Vegas, NV

"I like the easy-to-use format! This book allows the reader time to think to take their best action." ~ M. E. Hollywood, FL
"Wow, this is a real work of art. I cannot wait to get a copy! ~ Q. D. Houston, TX

"I love all the great information. I believe this will be a very helpful tool for many traders just starting out. Patience is the key to successful trading." ~ K. S., Tampa, FL

I would like to personally thank Angie A., from Pro_ebookcovers for designing the BEST cover EVER for this book, the PIP$, PROFIT$ & POWER Mindset Mastery Journal (and all my other books)!

I would personally like to thank by blessed editor, Cindy D. who let me know, that the content is wonderful! I LOVE that you are empowering women to change their financial situation. You are right... single women in their golden years are nearly destitute as a population! Well done, and I wish you all the best getting this out into the hands of women everywhere!

"Life is not measured by the number of breaths we take, but by the moments that take our breath away."
~~Anonymous

FOREX MINDSET MASTERY INTRODUCTION

""There is great power in letting go, and there is great FREEDOM in moving on."
~~Author Unknown

You have in your hands one of the BEST tools you will need to help you Master your Mindset to be a sustained, accomplished FOREX trader. In the past, your thoughts established your feelings and experiences about money, finances, bills, wealth, and prosperity. The past is in your head. This is the most significant reason why Mindset Mastery is vital for the FOREX trader. These past thoughts became your financial actions, creating your financial situations. The cumulative consequences of those financial situations are how you approach your finances today.

This Mindset will continue unless it is changed. The idea that life is tough and there is "not enough" plagues many. For most workers in the United States of America, $400 a month in addition to their salary, would allow them to sleep better at night and to begin saving and investing to make their money grow. Is this you?

Some thoughts that may have come to you about FOREX trading are:

All my trades will be profitable…
All the time.
I will make bundles of money doing this FAST!
This is easy.
I am a better trader than anyone else.
When I win, I feel good.
When I lose, I feel horrible.

These thoughts will not help make your FOREX trading journey any easier. In fact, these are the thoughts that could make your journey a complete failure. WOW! Make no mistake, FOREX trading has been known to leave losing trades and traders in its wake. EVERY. SINGLE. DAY. So, how do you Master your Mindset to keep your FOREX trading journey on the road to success, to live a life of Abundant Gratitude?

> *"The difference between winning and losing*
> *is most often not quitting."*
> *~~Walt Disney*

I came to a point in my life after many years of teaching special needs children that I wanted to learn something new. I knew so little in the beginning, I had to ask all about FOREX trading. I wanted to be able to have a little extra money as we began our lifestyle of Abundant Gratitude. So, I dove right in. I made my first trade about six days later with the help of a great number of wonderful people.

I realized in a short quick minute that FOREX trading had found me at a perfect time in my life. I could learn how to trade. So, I looked for a journal to get me started. When I found there was no Journal based on Mindset Mastery, it was a match made in heaven. Writing and trading have been my life ever since. I decided to do small things in a GREAT way to assist my fellow traders.

> *"If you cannot do great things,*
> *do small things in a GREAT way."*
> *~~Napoleon Hill*

I spoke to many newer FOREX Traders as I spent almost two years completing this Journal. Many wished they would have had something like this to get their journey started on the right foot, (interpreted as "started with a Mastered Mindset"). Clearly, your interest in FOREX trading is important to you.

Your desire to learn the skill of FOREX trading will hopefully be enhanced as you find points that you need to enrich your trading experience. Each trader is different. Your journey will be different too. Thanks so much for purchasing PIP$, PROFIT$ & POWER FOREX Mindset Mastery. Pairing this with the matching PIP$, PROFIT$ & POWER FOREX Journal will personalize and perfect your journey as you become a success and live a lifestyle of Abundant Gratitude.

> *"Tell me and I forget.*
> *Teach me and I remember.*
> *Involve me and I LEARN."*
> *~~Benjamin Franklin*

CHAPTER 1: MINDSET MASTERY, BELIEF & CONFIDENCE BUILDING

"WHAT WOULD YOU DO IF YOU KNEW YOU COULD NOT FAIL?"
~~Robert S. Schueller

Mindset Mastery is ultimately the skill of mastering your mindset, (your thoughts), for the task of successful FOREX trading. For some it may mean a full and complete "mindset makeover". Others may only need to change a few harmful thoughts to impact their FOREX trading outcomes. Mindset Mastery is vital when maintaining the single responsibility of the trader.

A FOREX trader has only one responsibility: *to protect the money in their live funded trading accounts*. Mindset Mastery may sound simple but can also be one of the most difficult things a trader must do. Mindset Mastery is what separates the successful traders from the quitters.

FOREX trading is the active action of buying or selling currency pairs. The foreign exchange market determines the foreign exchange rates worldwide moment by moment. All aspects of buying, selling, and exchanging currencies are determined in this market. FOREX traders include central banks, corporations, institutional investors, banks and individual traders. Markets are balanced, international trade and tourism are all facilitated by FOREX trading.

Regardless which entity places FOREX trades, positions are placed for a specific or a variety of reasons. The Central Banks, corporations and institutions place FOREX orders to move markets and set the prices of the currencies. Most individuals trade simply to make a personal profit. They do this by learning how to trade in the FOREX market on their own. Some learn in a very formal setting like a college or university. Others learn in a less formal setting like their home, through a course on the Internet.

> *"Change your thoughts and you change the world."*
> *~~Norman Vincent Peale*

Mindset Mastery begins with a belief in yourself. How can you trust that you will succeed? You have observed others becoming successful traders before you, so you know it is possible, but how do you know you will be successful with FOREX trading? Personal belief in yourself is a journey that builds this confidence. The trading venture you have chosen can build a fortune to define your legacy. Your personal beliefs and confidence will determine if you're going to be among the most successful traders.

Personal belief is born from within. The steps from personal belief to "ALL OUT" confidence will become your journey when there is honesty and truth. Be honest with yourself. Listen to what you are saying, what you do, and what you think about before, during and after any trade. What do you review each day to strengthen your confidence before you trade?

How you mold and plan your daily trading interactions will end up shaping how the rest of your day or week plays out. How deeply do you believe in yourself, in the concepts and strategies of successful trading you are applying as you trade? Take control of what you believe you can do and why you are focused on Forex trading to master your mindset for the success you so desire.

Your personal belief builds confidence when daily learning and practice are implemented regularly into your trading experience. Daily learning and practice will sustain you. Regular trading will build consistency while you trade. Building your confidence will allow you to avoid becoming dependent on those who share their trading details.

It is very easy to simply copy the trades of others. However, until you can confidently enter and execute successful trades on your own, how confident will you be in your own skills as a trader?

The following basics will assist with personal belief building, develop your consistently improving skills, and to strengthen your self-confidence for profitable successful FOREX trades.

> *"Nothing is impossible. The word it's-self says*
> *"I'm possible"."*
> *~~Audrey Hepburn*

FOREX education is about obtaining knowledge about currency pair matches, to reinforce belief in the FOREX market and to build consistent personal confidence. Focusing on your WHY, applying daily learning and skill development, makes it possible for your brain to calmly see what the market is presenting to you. Your belief can build rock solid confidence when tapping the unlimited potential within the $500 billion FOREX market. Everything you have learned and applied about FOREX creates an environment where your dreams are possible.

The first and the most important of the basics is to identify WHY you want to become a FOREX trader in the first place. Trading without knowing your WHY will impact how rapidly you build your account, because knowing your why allows the universe to act in your favor to assist you in meeting your goals and dreams. Determining which new skills should be applied to the next trades will build Mindset Mastery the fastest, especially with the less experienced trader.

Profitable trading starts with the proper Mindset just like anything else you put your mind to. Take time to learn your WHY and write it down. Review your WHY statement daily to keep you on track. At some point a review of that statement may signal it is time for you to modify your WHY statement. This is an indication of growth. Practice trading every day the market is open. This will keep your skills keen and sharp and will make a real difference in your FOREX Mindset towards Mastery. The best mentors will tell you, "The money is in building your skills daily.".

---

*"People don't buy what you do,
they buy WHY you do it."
~ Simon Sinek*

The second basic is finding a mentor. Stay connected to those who trade successfully every day. Online trading can be very isolating, however finding a mentor or trading group can help alleviate this. A mentor, Master Trader or trading group may be offered by those who introduced you to trading, or others who mentor may be able to help.

Your mentor should match your personality and meaningfully engage you in the way you learn best. Ask and find those who provide ongoing support, and training, but also have the desire for those they mentor to become independent mentors themselves and provide the level of support that best helps you meet your trading goals.

As you start, practice FOREX trading in a Demo account. In many cases you can learn from those who have forged the trading trail before you. Use the information they share to build your belief as you practice trading in your Demo account. In the beginning, much of your trading time should be spent in your Demo account, as this is an excellent space to try out a new strategy or idea. As your skills are sharpened and you modify trading to your personal levels of accomplishment and comfort, the time to trade live will arrive!

Learn from those who inspire you. Imitate what they did to become successful FOREX traders and follow their instructions, suggestions and directions to the letter! A past mentor referred to this skill as "recharging the batteries". Frequent recharging of your batteries will need to come from somewhere, especially after a large loss. Recycle mentoring from your notes, to spur momentum for ongoing success and skill application.

"One way to keep momentum going is to have constantly greater goals."
~~Michael Korda

The next important basic is to create Grounded Trading Goals. Grounded Trading Goals are best when written down. Written goals have proven to be massively more effective than goals which are not written down. Some studies indicate that written goals have a 42% better chance of being met than unwritten goals. This fact indicates that when goals are written down, there is an almost 1 in 2 chance that they will be met! When we are talking about FOREX trades, would you take a 42% better chance of success?

Give yourself the necessary time to learn the vocabulary, determine your favorite pair, your favorite system and all the indicators that will make you the most successful. Continue to write progressive goals that detail your desires and ambitions to match your WHY and your Prosperity Trading Plan. Include every aspect of your learning into your goals if necessary.

The process of goal writing is personal for each one of us. When writing goals some prefer the SMART method while others choose to just put their words to paper. Either way, FOREX trading goals do need to be measurable, attainable, and realistic. The goals should be measurable, so you are aware when they have been achieved. Writing goals that work for you is a skill that can be used for a lifetime.

> *"A goal without a plan is just a wish."*
> *~~Antoine de Saint-Exupery*

    The next basic is to create a Prosperity Trading Plan. A prosperity plan is not a schedule. A Trading Prosperity Plan is a description of what you want to accomplish each day and over time, with specific components.

    Your schedule is used to place all the day's activity into a format to make sure you are on time for the other appointments and commitments in your life, including trading times. This may be determined for you by those you love and care for and/or who cares for you. Does your lifestyle most match the New York session or the London session? Once you know, you can match this timing about when you will be trading with the outline of the Compounding Interest sheet.

> *"Challenges are what make life interesting and overcoming*
> *them is what makes life meaningful."*
> *~~ Joshua J. Marine*

    A Prosperity Plan includes a plan for your trading, to be all it can be for your lifestyle desires and wishes. Your personal wealth planning and timing is a critical part of your Prosperity Trading Plan. Most include their other sources of wealth and income into their Prosperity Plan to make it more complete and revealing allowing space for both financial limitations and allowances f or trading.

    Unbreakable Trading Rules. YES. Unbreakable. This basic is the "diamond in the paper bag" that will best protect the money in your FOREX funded account. These rules must be so solid, there is nothing that will allow you to enter a trade without them.

    Possibly, the system you have chosen will have trading rules built in. In that case, all you need to do is ensure you can identify your Unbreakable Trading Rules, be able to state them and DO NOT enter trades in which the rules may be broken.

    As I completed my research for this book and the companion Journal, I spoke with many newer traders. Repeatedly, there were three things they mentioned. The first, for these FOREX traders, was the inability to be able to identify high-probability trades. The second was how to properly identify appropriate or "exact" entry. The third was when to exit a trade, both in loss and in profit. The answers to these questions are heavily dependent on your *PERSONAL COMFORT AND RELATIONSHIP WITH YOUR MONEY.* These questions also rely upon the type of trader you are, on the amount in your trading account, and the desired number of pips or dollars to be earned for the trading session. The answers must be found by each successful trader.

"Strength doesn't come from what you can do. It comes from overcoming the things you thought you couldn't do."
~~Rikki Rodgers

Trade Entry Indicators are a basic that most newer traders rely heavily on. Trade Entry Indicators may prevent a great deal of heartache. Sometimes, when listening to my mentors they indicated that the market needs to move in a certain way to confirm the direction of the next high-probability trade. When I applied their advice, I could see that the market had not made that move and I realized the move may not come for a couple of hours, days or even weeks. Then, I learned how to trade differently. If the trader is not patient, and instead jumps right in, drawdown or consolidation might be experienced first. This could result in the loss of funding and to the disappointment of the trader, the funding in the account was not protected.

Entry Indicators can easily be included when using a trading checklist. Once it is used for a short period of time, the indicators will be easily recalled. In the beginning the checklist will be an invaluable tool to ensure the trades are entering and exiting FOREX trades according to your training, ability and comfort. Experience will help modify and mold the checklist for the most successful trades as time goes by.

"The great aim of education is not knowledge but action,"
~~Herbert Spencer

Daily FOREX Learning is the single basic that any trader can most control. The trader is the sole person who determines how much learning is necessary to apply to improve the monetary outcomes of each of the trading positions. Daily learning is necessary to increase individual trading skills, vocabulary, strategies and techniques needed to trade independently and with others.

Those who teach Forex trading must continue to learn. All training venues have knowledge. Knowledge you may need for tomorrow, can be found today. Someone once told me, "You should spend up to 2 hours a day educating yourself, because the knowledge you gain on your own cannot be replicated anywhere else". Some team leaders have created training sites that could have valuable information also. Knowing where the information can be found is the beginning of knowing how to apply it.

"He who dares to teach,
never ceases to learn."
~~John Colton Dana

A personal unmatched Passion for trading may have already developed all on its own. Typically, the passion for a new endeavor or "something NEW to do", appears as frantic energy on fire! Having an experience with someone who has found how to be rich in "10 minutes" makes most of us want to run for our lives. We know that this frantic expression of their passion and excitement will probably be short lived, as they may burn out quickly. Those who are more experienced know that this level of energy is not sustainable.

For those who will eventually develop a life-long passion for FOREX trading, their energy is funneled into following steps to build their skills and confidence every day. These traders are focused on skill building like generating unbreakable rules or specific entry indicators. Realizing the power of a trend and following it will increase your passion for targeting your awareness of profitable trades with lower risk.

"Your passion is waiting for your
courage to catch up."
~~ Isabelle Lafleche

The feelings experienced at the end of the most successful trades, with actual measurable results, are very exciting. This could pave the parking lot of the mansion, make the payment on your luxury car, or the down payment on your next vacation home. Doors open doors. Passion is a very good thing… OR is it? So, when does passion for FOREX trading become TRADER'S GREED?

GREED is the biggest downfall of the trader.

FOREX trading is not a way to get rich quick. You must know what you are doing with a funded account. Holding onto a trade that brings you into the blue and beyond, makes a trader feel like they're walking on air! Likewise, if a pair keeps hitting the stop loss, or the account is blown, it could make a trader feel like the sky is falling and some very strong negative feelings could develop. Many quit! When they do, their goals and dreams are dashed.

When it feels like you've already realized the profits before you really begin, you could be in trouble. Yes, there is prosperity and wealth in great belief. But the markets are eager to take your money. Fear of missing out or FOMO makes the trader sell too soon. GREED makes the trader hold on too long. Once the financial goal has been met for the day….

STOP TRADING!

"He who is GREEDY is always in want."
~ Horace

The next basic is Responsible Risk Management. Yes, it is one of the first things FOREX traders hear about but may be one of the HARDEST lessons learned, at a much later date. This basic is the one that allows for a $5,000 initial account to be built to a $32,000 account in a matter of months. Learning how a ".01" risk can earn money is critical to the FOREX trader. Not having the type of patience needed to build slowly may mean that you will have to stop trading and to save to start all over again. Remember taking care of the money in your account? What did inspired trading teach you today that strengthened your mindset? This is a gem of the FOREX Mindset that needs to be Mastered!

> *"Risk comes from not knowing
> what you are doing."*
> *~~Warren Buffet*

How did you learn what you need to know NEXT in order to protect the money in your account and to build upon it each trading session? Could it be a $10.00 trade? Maybe it's a $100 decision to stay in a trade in the red? Maybe it's $1,000,000 trade shared with your trading group in the future. These lessons don't need to be costly to your account. It is always recommended that you practice your chosen market strategy with a demo account before you attempt greater risk with your real FOREX trading account.

The most successful traders have discovered how to use a simple compound interest chart. This chart allows you to understand how money multiplies if the chart is followed. This is the same chart that is used for those who offer "payday" or very short-term lending. When on the paying side of this chart… it is virtually impossible to catch up. When on the earning side of this chart, the potential is unlimited.

Enlist those who you trust to assist you in making your online trading experience a phenomenal success. Use the tools you have been given. Traders who follow reasonable and responsible risk management will find that they are able to secure the money in their accounts and to better understand the risk to reward ratio. Identify the tools that indicate the lowest risk trades. Learn about Compound Interest and apply it to your trades. Find a Compounding Interest chart on the Internet.

> *"Most great fortunes are built slowly.
> They are built on the principle of compound interest."*
> *~~Brian Tracy*

Journaling will work better if it is ongoing, or very consistent if you are a newer trader. This FOREX trading journey will be more successful as you Master your Mindset. Joyful Journaling is a personal task which provides you words and numbers to complete your trading story. Use your journal to provide you information only your trading journal can provide. Joyful Journaling and Authentic Trading go hand in hand. Journaling has been found to contribute to personal belief and growth. Keep an accounting of your trades. This helps the trader to understand how much is being earned and how much may be being lost.

Write STUFF down. Seems easy, but many traders do not journal their trades, the parts of FOREX education that is working for them, or how they are feeling about the trading process. What are the spreads costing you? Should you change brokers at a certain point, so your costs are lower? Without having a record to identify these costs or how much lower risk trades you are taking over time, mistakes could be made. Use your PIP$. PROFIT$ & POWER Journal FOREX Mindset Mastery to write your successful trading story!

"Don't practice until you get it right,
Practice until you can't get it wrong."
~~Unknown

The practice of FOREX Trading Authentically uses the tools you have been given to create an ongoing environment of success. Authentic trading consists of understanding why you are entering a trade, how long you plan to stay in and what conditions will be necessary for you to exit successfully. Authentic trading also includes when you will trade again and WHY.

Is a trade that ends in a loss a successful trade? Many may not think so, however others believe the answer is YES. Why? Because, when lessons are learned the first time through, they may not easily be repeated. However, lessons not learned can lead to repeated mistakes. Not caring about any single component of the trading process will impact how you trade.

"Happiness lies in the joy of achievement and the thrill of creative effort."
~~Franklin D. Roosevelt

One of the final basics is taking responsibility for your actions. To become your best in your trading journey, you must take responsibility for yourself. What does it take to be your best? Can you ask for help when you need it? As adults we don't like to admit that we might need help to show us the way to the top. Take responsibility and ask questions of your mentor or even of your broker will help you when you need it.

Trying to find your way to the financial end you desire, without knowing the way it is no different than an ill-advised trip to the beach. This could be much more expensive, not only financially, but emotionally and motivationally too. Protect your Mindset as you would your trading account.

The best way to take responsibility for your actions is to follow your trading goals, trading prosperity plan and most importantly your Unbreakable Trading Rules to the letter. These become the best way to protect your account, the best way to have a successful trading story and to know what your next move is and how to place the next AWESOME profitable trade. That is POWER!

"If you take responsibility for yourself, you will develop a hunger to accomplish your dreams."
~~Les Brown

Last, is visualization for your success, dreams and living in abundance. Now's the time to visualize where you want your FOREX trading journey to take you whether you may be ready to take the first step in this FOREX trading journey or have traded for a while. Trading can be confusing, frustrating and expensive at best.

If you don't know where you're going, it's like standing on the beach looking out upon the ocean, intending to swim across. With the water splashing gently on your toes, it does seem possible. All you see is water expanding below your feet in both directions and straight in front of you. No matter how bright the sunshine, no matter how enticing the trading market may be, the trading journey before you could seem equally as overwhelming to you at this point.

"There is WISDOM of the head and WISDOM of the heart."
~~Charles Dickens

However, if you step back 50 feet or more on the beach, suddenly you can see and experience the beach, but in a much different way. Listen to the sound of eternal waves gently washing the sand at water's edge. The water may appear to have more contrasting colors and your toes may no longer be wet, instead they are caked with wet sand. There may appear to be more humanity around you, although they were there from the start. Smell the seafood from that nearby restaurant? What changed?

Perspective. Perspective is all in how we see what is right in front of us. Perspective is seeing what the market has served us, much like when we look out at the weather. We can take what we see and dress accordingly, or either be too hot or too cold for the day. Trading is the same thing. We must apply our rules and see if they match the "weather" we have been given. If not, it could be a very cold or a very hot day!

"Life is about perspective and how you look at something…
ultimately, you have to zoom out."
~~Whitney Wolf Herd

So, it is never too late to be your best and take your trading journey to the next level. Don't wait any longer. Find the information that will allow you to move forward. What links did you miss that someone else has shared, but you never looked up? Study how those who are where you perceive you want to be, did it themselves. If it was done once, it can be done and repeated as many times as it takes.

Make prosperity plans to drive to the mansion, become a test driver of the car. Find an investment in others that is bigger than you. Look past the doors to see what else is waiting for you there. Waiting for tomorrow may not seem like it will matter, but you may realize months later that you are months behind traders who stayed with trading day after day, and this will delay your BIG Dreams. Figure out if FOREX trading is not for you. Don't let your gifts to go unrealized.

CHALLENGE 1: Belief & Confidence
*"Choose a job you love, and you will
never work a day in your life."
~~Confucius*

PROFITS Affirmation: My CHOICES got me where I am today, and my CHOICES will take me somewhere new.

POWER Word: CHOICES

My Affirmation:
_____
_____

Profitable Trading Wisdom: List the messages you heard most often growing up. Comment on how those messages formed your CHOICES.

_____
_____
_____
_____
_____
_____
_____
_____
_____
_____
_____
_____
_____
_____
_____

CHALLENGE 2: Belief & Confidence
"There are no limitations to the mind except those we acknowledge."
~~Napoleon Hill

PROFITS Affirmation: Today, I release the LIMITATIONS that no longer serve me.

POWER Word: LIMITATIONS

My Affirmation:
_____
_____

Profitable Trading Wisdom: List the LIMITATIONS that may be holding me back from profitable trading.

_____
_____
_____
_____
_____
_____
_____
_____
_____
_____
_____
_____
_____
_____

CHALLENGE 3: Belief & Confidence
"If we did all the things, we are capable of doing, we would astound ourselves."
~~Thomas Edison

PROFITS Affirmation: Today, I ASTOUND myself with all I am capable of.

POWER Word: ASTOUND

My Affirmation:
_____
_____

Profitable Trading Wisdom: List the 5 experiences that most ASTOUND you in your life.

_____
_____
_____
_____
_____
_____
_____
_____
_____
_____
_____
_____
_____
_____
_____
_____
_____
_____

CHALLENGE 4: Belief & Confidence
"Ninety~nine percent of all failures come from people who have a habit of making excuses."
~~George Washington Carver

PROFITS Affirmation: Today, I choose a HABIT of no excuses.

POWER Word: HABIT

My Affirmation:
_____
_____

Profitable Trading Wisdom: List 10 of your positive habits. List 1 HABIT you will be working on to change.

_____
_____
_____
_____
_____
_____
_____
_____
_____
_____
_____
_____
_____
_____
_____
_____

CHALLENGE 5: Belief & Confidence
"The number one problem that keeps people from
winning… is lack of belief in themselves."
~~A. L. Williams

PROFITS Affirmation: I BELIEVE in myself.

POWER Word: BELIEVE

My Affirmation:
_____
_____

Profitable Trading Wisdom: Describe how you BELIEVE in yourself in new ways (like you haven't believed before).

CHAPTER 2: FOCUS ON WHY

---

*"Charisma has nothing to do with energy; it comes from a clarity of WHY.
It comes from absolute conviction in an ideal bigger than oneself."*
~~Simon Sinek, Start with Why, p. 133

Time is the only currency which cannot be traded, purchased or saved. It therefore is the most precious and should be treasured. Money on the other hand, is another story. Back when stones or coins or furs were used to trade, they were given a value, just as our fiat currency, the dollar is today. When it comes to our dollars, it is most important to protect the dollars we already have. Avoid scams which take your dollars without providing you a real service. The best services provide an educational payback. Paying for knowledge will always be with you as no one can take the information from you. Invest in yourself!

WHY is the most important question you can answer for yourself!

As you make your decision to trade FOREX, deep down inside each trader there is a reason WHY. Hopefully, your WHY is deep enough to help or assist others. Clarity of the trader's WHY will make the process of trading Authentic. A mentor once said that if your "WHY doesn't make you cry..." then it is not strong or powerful enough. Take some of your most precious currency, time, to question and clarify your deepest reasons WHY you desire to become a trader. This will enhance your trading experience and make you a better trader over time.

"There is no stupid question."
~~Unknown

Those who saw your potential and shared the FOREX journey with you did so because they cared about you. These supportive entrepreneurs are not looking for millionaires, they are looking for someone who has your skillset and temperament. The potential they saw was a part of their own personal WHY. Maybe they wanted to help you realize a dream. Maybe their own dream is bigger than both of you, and your recruitment will fulfill more in you than you know. Regardless of their reason for sharing, their WHY came with a motivation and momentum which can be carried into your endeavor as the spark to get you going.

There are those who realized people would pay hard earned cash for rocks with faces painted on them, rubber bands that come in animal shapes and dolls which have adoption papers. They realized these things represent a "cash cow". Each one of these successful ventures had a WHY that was well stated. The best analysis can earn you enormous profits or take hard earned profits away quickly. FOREX trading is not much different. Treating your newly acquired skills as a business proposition is not a bad idea, considering the money that will be invested for your FOREX education and to fund your live trading accounts.

> *"Some men see things as they are and ask WHY?*
> *Others dreams things that*
> *never were, and ask WHY not?"*
> *~~George Bernard Shaw*

Workplace relationships can become "Business Partners" or "Friends" who are there to support you. These relationships help mold and form our futures. These are the relationships which could impact your dreams, bank account, and possibly your retirement. Your career or your goal to learn trading could depend on these relationships. For some, the workplace is the fulfillment of their WHY, and your desire to share FOREX may be perceived as inappropriate. It is important to respect the workplace to maintain a professional climate and culture.

One mentor I respected said, "Don't let the person who thought so much of you… DOWN". So, don't. Maintain the qualities of producing high-quality work, displaying a positive attitude, and treating others the way you want to be treated. These are mindful actions that unleash the power of a leader.

Powerful leaders are focused, committed, passionate, persistent, innovative, and active. Practice a life without limits, realizing what is truly possible. Plan for your supporters to open the doors to your mansion, ride in your new car or take vacations with you! Their consistent celebrations are the fulfillment of their sharing with you and the realization of your potential with FOREX. Allow your greatness to shine!

> *"The person who says it cannot be done should not be interrupted by the person who is doing it."*
> *~~Chinese Proverb*

There will be those who detract from your energy and efforts and who will question your WHY. They are the "Dream Stealers", the "Debbie Downers" and the "Vision Vixens". They could be a spouse, a best friend or a family member. When you realize that they are in your life, do not try to include convincing them as part of your WHY. This is a waste of energy, and a waste of valuable time.

Don't let these detractors interrupt you from awakening the potential with in you. Clarify your WHY to stay focused. Instead, concentrate on how much effort it will take to see your dreams come true, in-spite of the discouragement they spread. Are you an extraordinary leader who is not able to lead in the position you are in? Listen to your heart.

More than anything else, know life is way too short to stay in a job you dislike or hate. If not, there are other opportunities out there which could interest you. Find them and get started without delay. As you focus on your WHY, you will come to understand if FOREX trading is indeed for you.

> *"It is never too late to be what you might have been."*
> *~~George Eliot*

Keeping secrets from those you love, about money, is never recommended and nothing makes loved ones prouder of your efforts than when you realize success. Purchasing an expensive dress or a pair of jeans is not nearly as hard to explain to someone you love, as is money invested in FOREX trading without much return or great loss, especially when as a newer trader, warnings were not heeded.

Help these loved ones understand that helping others gets them what others want and then YOU get what you want. Include this in your WHY and you will discover a life you never imagined. Become what you were meant to be.

The FOREX story you will tell for years will begin with a single moment. Love yourself first to reduce your stress. By defining your WHY, you will also find clarity for your beliefs, what you want, feelings, confidence, dreams, commitments and actions.

> *"When you feel like quitting,*
> *remember WHY you started."*
> *~~John di lemme*

This moment is like few others in your life. One example is the moment you decided what to major in once you decided to attend college. From that day forward you always will see the world through that lens, i.e. education or medicine. Another is the first day you fell in love.

You will always measure all other similar encounters on that experience. This moment in your FOREX trading journey is similar. Your life will not be the same once you have clarity about your personal WHY, and your FOREX trading WHY..

> *"You are about to come into a season where you are about to experience breakthrough after breakthrough because what you've been through didn't BREAK you."*
> *~~Unknown*

MY PERSONAL WHY STATEMENT

A WHY statement should provide answers about your beliefs, wants, feelings, future, dreams, commitments and actions.

When I think about becoming a FOREX Trader, I BELIEVE I am on this earth…
to _____
_____

When I think about becoming a FOREX Trader, I WANT…
to _____
_____

for _____
_____

When I think about being a FOREX Trader, I FEEL…
_____
_____

When I think about being a FOREX Trader, MY CONFIDENCE…
_____
_____

When I think about being a FOREX Trader, MY LIFE'S DREAMS…
_____
_____

When I think about being a FOREX Trader, I COMMIT TO…
_____
_____

When I think about being a FOREX Trader, I WILL DO…
_____
_____

> *"A Friend knows the song in my heart*
> *and sings it to me when my memory fails."*
> *~~Unknown*

CHALLENGE 6: WHY
*"The indispensable first step to getting the things you want
out of life is this: decide what you want."*
~~Ben Stein

PROFITS Affirmation: I have DECIDED what I want.

POWER Word: DECIDED

My Affirmation:
_____
_____

Profitable Trading Wisdom: Describe how you DECIDED what you want. (Be Specific.)

_____
_____
_____
_____
_____
_____
_____
_____
_____
_____
_____
_____
_____
_____
_____

CHALLENGE 7: WHY

"Knowing your WHY is not the only way to be successful, but it is the only way to maintain a lasting success and have a greater blend of innovation and flexibility."
~~Simon Sinek, Start with WHY p. 50

PROFITS Affirmation: Today, I know my WHY, I now have greater INNOVATION and flexibility.

POWER Word: INNOVATION

My Affirmation:
_____
_____

Profitable Trading Wisdom: I maintain lasting success; I have greater INNOVATION and flexible because…

_____
_____
_____
_____
_____
_____
_____
_____
_____
_____
_____
_____
_____
_____

CHALLENGE 8: WHY?
"Riches begin with a state of mind, with a definiteness of purpose."
~~Napoleon Hill

PROFITS Affirmation: My WHY and my state of mind, have a definite PURPOSE to build my riches!

POWER Word: PURPOSE

My Affirmation:
_____
_____

Profitable Trading Wisdom: Write about how your state of mind impacts your PURPOSE.

_____
_____
_____
_____
_____
_____
_____
_____
_____
_____
_____
_____
_____
_____
_____

CHALLENGE 9: WHY

"When we are selective about doing business only with those who believe in our WHY, trust emerges."
~~Simon Sinek, Start with Why p. 80

PROFITS Affirmation: I TRUST FOREX partners will come to me to support my belief in my WHY.

POWER Word: TRUST

My Affirmation:
_____
_____

Profitable Trading Wisdom: I TRUST the FOREX partners in my life because...

_____
_____
_____
_____
_____
_____
_____
_____
_____
_____
_____
_____
_____
_____

CHALLENGE 10: WHY

"The two most important days of your life are the day you were born and the day you find out WHY."
~~Mark Twain

PROFITS Affirmation: I have FOUND and am ready to write my WHY.

POWER Word: FOUND

My Affirmation:
_____
_____

Profitable Trading Wisdom: Describe how you FOUND your WHY.

CHAPTER 3: CONSISTENT CONFIDENCE & MENTORING

"Too many people overvalue what they are not and UNDERVALUE what they are."
~~Malcolm S. Forbes

CONSISTENT CONFIDENCE

C ~ Courage   *+ C ~ Consideration* = *Concrete Beliefs*
O ~ Original   *+ O ~ Opportunity* = *Optimistic WHY*
N ~ Necessity *+ N ~ Nerve* = *Necessary Mentoring*
S ~ Stability *+ F ~ Faith* = *Strong Factual Goals*
I ~ Integrity *+ I ~ Intact* = *Ideal Intact Plan*
S ~ Solid   *+ D ~ Dignity* = *Safe Daring Rules*
T ~ Tenacity *+ E ~ Education* = *Trade Expertise*
E ~ Endure   *+ N ~ Need* = *Proper Risk Management*
N ~ Natural *+ C ~ Currency* = *Noted Care Journal*
T ~ Timely   *+ E ~ Envision* = *Thriving Expectation*

*"For every achievement, there is a price.
For every goal, there is an opponent.
For every victory, there is a problem.
For every triumph, there is a sacrifice."*
~~William Arthur Ward

If you found a gap in your skills or in your courage, an appropriate mentor could assist you. Your willingness to learn and as you apply new knowledge, most likely there will be more questions. Your willingness to be coached and mentored will bring you to better leadership. Make sure you know what you are looking for and can communicate that as you interview a potential mentor. Excellent mentorship could bring the shyest of FOREX traders to become excellent mentors themselves! Mentorship is an acquired skill.

"Knowledge is knowing what to say,
wisdom is knowing when to say it."
~~Anonymous

How do you find an excellent mentor who matches your skillset and personality? An interview is always a good idea. Ask the questions that most interest you when you are about to work with someone new. The interview could consist of simply listening. Your mentor interview must include the questions you found when you clarified your WHY.

Remember your time, energy and money is at stake here. Choose well and if you are not satisfied... change! If what you hear does not sit well with you, obviously, that person may not be a good mentor for you. However, the questions you ask a potential mentor should be both professional and personal. Write them out first.

"Winners never quit, and quitters never win."
~~Vince Lombardi

Every person begins a new endeavor with a mustard seed of courage. Your WHY may have helped you clarify what may be missing for you to realize success. The answers to your WHY questions could be the elements which unlock the perseverance you will need to continue to trade and mentorship could be vital to your success. A strong mentor will share wisdom and gracefully lead the new FOREX trader to experience success. Some who come to FOREX have come by way of a network marketing program. The person who sponsored you may not necessarily be the person who would be your best mentor.

Not quitting is really the difference between winning and losing (not money) in FOREX. Be perfectly honest with yourself, about your WHY, trading, and what you are looking for from your mentor. Your ability to be coached is something you must be very honest about. This is difficult for many adults. There are adults who are looking for a mentor and others may be looking for a "babysitter" or "hand-holder". Mentorship becomes a workable relationship in a very short amount of time, or it may not develop.

The information you receive from your mentor should drive you to educate yourself to choose high-probability trades that have an appropriate risk to reward ratio. You must be able to identify proper risk management and apply it as soon as possible. Allow your mentor to coach you so that you will not be a "copy-cat trader", a trader who cannot determine if a trade should be placed unless it comes from someone else. This is a great barrier to becoming a successful trader.

"Success is measured by your discipline and inner peace."
~~Mike Ditka

Not taking responsibility for taking ill-advised trades is not the responsibility of your mentor. Blaming and not properly communicating your thoughts and feelings will keep your mentoring relationship and FOREX journey from moving forward. Take responsibility. It is rewarding and allows the trader to gain courage with each trade. This discipline and inner peace will allow the trader to protect the balance in their account.

You may desire to become a mentor yourself. There are professional courses, that teach mentoring. Choose what matches the type of FOREX mentoring you plan to do. There are those who are naturally able to mentor and lead others. These are the best and of course have the most followers. Be mindful of their time. Savvy leadership is demonstrated when leaders have a combination of excellent skills.

These leaders connect within the moment, identify a need with powerful questions, listen, remain focused, act when requested and to review the leadership process to celebrate all the success. Inspiration and direction are necessary to ensure that both the mentor and the mentee are progressing, bravely challenging each other while celebrating joint success.

"Mentoring is a brain to pick, an ear to listen and
a push in the right direction."
~~John Crosby

CHALLENGE 11: Consistent Confidence & Mentoring

"The greater danger for most of us is not that our aim is too high, and we miss it, but that we aim too low and we reach it."

~~Michelangelo

PROFITS Affirmation: I AIM high enough as I dream of becoming a successful FOREX trader.

POWER Word: AIM

My Affirmation:

_____

_____

Profitable Trading Wisdom: Describe your highest AIM with FOREX trading.

CHALLENGE 12: Consistent Confidence & Mentoring

"Life will always give you feedback about the effects of your behavior if you will just pay attention."
~~Jack Canfield

PROFITS Affirmation: I pay attention to the FEEDBACK my life provides about the effects of my behavior.

POWER Word: FEEDBACK

My Affirmation:
_____
_____

Profitable Trading Wisdom: List the FEEDBACK you have received about your behavior and share how that created an opportunity for you.

_____
_____
_____
_____
_____
_____
_____
_____
_____
_____
_____
_____
_____
_____
_____
_____

CHALLENGE 13: Consistent Confidence & Mentoring

"It isn't until you forgive what's in the past that you'll be able to receive the gift of the present."
~~Andy Andrews

PROFITS Affirmation: I FORGIVE myself for the past, holding onto grievances with others, which may affect my trading journey.

POWER Word: FORGIVE

My Affirmation:
_____
_____

Profitable Trading Wisdom: Comment on how you FORGIVE yourself.

CHALLENGE 14: Consistent Confidence & Mentoring
*"I have the will to do what others won't,
So, I can have what others don't."
~~Jeffery Combs*

PROFITS Affirmation: I am DOING what others won't, so I can have what others don't.

POWER Word: DOING

My Affirmation:
_____
_____

Profitable Trading Wisdom: What are 5 ways you are DOING what others won't to get what you want.

CHALLENGE 15: Consistent Confidence & Mentoring
"You either create or allow everything that happens to you."
~~Jack Canfield

PROFITS Affirmation: Today, I take the positive steps to CREATE the life I desire.

POWER Word: CREATE

My Affirmation:
_____
_____

Profitable Trading Wisdom: CREATE the next 5 positive future steps you plan to take towards successful trading.

CHALLENGE 16: Taking Responsibility

"Work on yourself first, take responsibility for your own progress."
~~I Ching

PROFITS Affirmation: I am 100% RESPONSIBLE for my own progress.

POWER Word: RESPONSIBLE

My Affirmation:
_____
_____

Profitable Trading Wisdom: List 4 ways you are RESPONSIBLE for your finances, wealth and prosperity.

_____
_____
_____
_____
_____
_____
_____
_____
_____
_____
_____
_____
_____
_____
_____
_____
_____
_____

CHALLENGE 17: Taking Responsibility
"If you want to be happy, set a goal that commands your thoughts, liberates your energy and inspires your hopes."
~~Andrew Carnegie

PROFITS Affirmation: I COMMAND my thoughts to liberate my energy and inspire my hopes.

POWER Word: COMMAND

My Affirmation:
_____
_____

Profitable Trading Wisdom: List 5 ways you COMMAND your thoughts to liberate your energy and inspire you for FOREX trading.

_____
_____
_____
_____
_____
_____
_____
_____
_____
_____
_____
_____
_____
_____
_____
_____
_____
_____

CHALLENGE 18: Taking Responsibility

"As you start on your journey of success, your goals should be attainable AND should push you outside your comfort zone."
~~Steve Harvey, Act Like a Success, p. 110

PROFITS Affirmation: I have STARTED on my journey of success.

POWER Word: STARTED

My Affirmation:

_____

_____

Profitable Trading Wisdom: You have gotten STARTED, now what? List your challenges and concerns.

CHALLENGE 19: Taking Responsibility
"Little minds are tamed and
subdued by misfortune,
but great minds rise above it."
~~Washington Irving

PROFITS Affirmation: Today, I rise above misfortune by using my great MIND.

POWER Word: MIND

My Affirmation:
_____
_____

Profitable Trading Wisdom: Discuss how you rise above misfortune to Master your MIND.

_____
_____
_____
_____
_____
_____
_____
_____
_____
_____
_____
_____
_____
_____
_____
_____

Challenge 20: Taking Responsibility
*"If you cannot see the possibility of greatness,
how can we dream it?"
~~Lee Strasburg*

PROFITS Affirmation: I see the possibility of my GREATNESS.

POWER Word: GREATNESS

My Affirmation:
_____
_____

Profitable Trading Wisdom: Discuss the possibilities of your GREATNESS.

CHAPTER 4: GROUNDED TRADING GOALS
*"My goal is not to be better than anyone else,
but to be better than I used to be."
~~Dr. Wayne Dyer*

Writing goals of any kind is usually a process, however, writing Grounded Trading Goals does not have to be. Some struggle with the process of writing goals, not because they are unable to put words to paper, but because there is fear of commitment. Putting words to paper means you will have to do something to attain them. Attaining your goals could mean that you are successful. Poor belief or not understanding your WHY has resulted in this lack of confidence. After taking a second look at your level of belief and your relationship to being successful, reviewing your WHY could be of great value.

When writing goals, make sure to identify a goal that can be met, but not too easily. Here is an example. To state a goal such as "to make more money" and your next trade earns $.26 profit, there has been "more money" earned. Obviously, this goal is attainable and very realistic, but may not match your WHY or your Prosperity Trading Plan because the goal is not descriptive enough to get you to the monetary level you desire. Writing goals increases your belief and confidence!

*"To handle Yourself, use your head.
To handle Others, use your heart."
~~Eleanor Roosevelt*

Some use the **SMART** method to write goals. This acronym stands for:

S = Specific	Specific enough to see the change
M = Measurable	Measurable enough to know there is change
A = Attainable	Attainable enough to be facilitated by you
R = Realistic	Realistic enough it could happen
T = Timely	Timely, the change happens over time

A more realistic goal would be to earn $100 four days in a row. In the same manner, earning a million dollars in the first year after you start with a $500 account may not be attainable or realistic. Being realistic and reasonable will keep you trading in the FOREX markets and will help you maintain your account balance. This proven method has been used repeatedly by those who are successful.

When writing goals, motivation is increased if the activity reflects your personality. Use materials to decorate the paper you have written on or use decorated paper. Add a few lines about how you will feel when the goals are met. Does the goal match your WHY? If not, tweak it. To ensure that your goals can be met share your goal to provide a level of responsibility and accountability. Right now, take an action step towards your goal immediately. The momentum you started as you put your words into the goal statement and your action step can propel you to the next goal.

Read your entire goal morning and night to build your belief and confidence. The remainder of the belief statement is adapted from Think and Grow Rich, by Napoleon Hill.

"By recording your dreams and goals on paper, you set in motion
the process of becoming the person you most want to be."
Put your future in good hands ~~ Your Own."
~~Mark Victor Hansen

A SAMPLE Grounded FOREX Trading GOAL: I am so happy and grateful now that…

By this specific date, I will be earning $8,500 per month trading FOREX. I know my goal is realistic because I am currently earning $2,000 per month trading FOREX.

I will measure this goal by using my compound interest chart for 2 months.

I know my goal is attainable because I am a successful FOREX trader who uses Responsible Risk Management.

My belief is so strong:
I believe I will earn this money.
I can see it with my eyes.
I can touch it with my hands.
In return for this money I will

_____

_____

_____

I will give up

_____

_____(space)in order to receive the money I earn.

It is now transferring to me as I deliver the service in return for it to the BEST of my ability.

Genie Craff

MY GROUNDED PERSONAL AND TRADING GOALS

---

*"The tragedy of life doesn't lie in
not reaching your goal.
The tragedy lies in having no goals to reach."*
~~Benjamin Mayes

My Grounded PERSONAL GOAL: I am so happy and grateful now that…

By _____, I will _____
_____

My goal is realistic
because_____
I will measure this goal
by _____
I know my goal is attainable
because _____

My belief is so strong:
I believe I will meet this goal.
I can see it with my eyes.
I can touch it with my hands.
In return for this goal I will
_____
I will give up
_____
_____in order to receive the money I earn.
It is now transferring to me as I deliver the service in return for it to the BEST of my ability.

NOTES:
_____
_____
_____

My Grounded FOREX Trading GOAL: I am so happy and grateful now that…
By _____, I will be earning
$_____/_____. I know my goal is realistic because…

_____
_____

I will measure this goal by…

_____
_____

I know my goal is attainable because…

_____
_____

To the BEST of my ability, my belief is so strong:
I believe I will earn this money.
I can see it with my eyes.
I can touch it with my hands.
In return for this money I will…

_____
_____
_____

I will give up…

_____
_____

in order to receive the money I earn.
The money is now transferring to me as I deliver the service in return for it.

My Next Grounded FOREX Trading GOAL: I am so happy and grateful now that…
By _____, I will be earning
$_____/_____. I know my goal is realistic because…
_____
_____

I will measure this goal by…
_____
_____

I know my goal is attainable because…
_____
_____

To the BEST of my ability, my belief is so strong:
I believe I will earn this money.
I can see it with my eyes.
I can touch it with my hands.
In return for this money I will… _____
_____
_____

I will give up…
_____
_____

in order to receive the money I earn. The money is now transferring to me as I deliver the service in return for it.

NOTES:
_____
_____
_____
_____
_____
_____
_____

CHALLENGE 21: Grounded Trading GOALS
"The BEST way to predict the future is to invent it."
~~Alan Kay

PROFITS Affirmation: I INVENT my future.

POWER Word: INVENT

My Affirmation:
_____
_____

Profitable Trading Wisdom: I INVENT my future when I.... Write 3 personal goals.

_____
_____
_____
_____
_____
_____
_____
_____
_____
_____
_____
_____
_____
_____
_____
_____
_____

CHALLENGE 22: Grounded Trading GOALS

*"The most creative act you will ever undertake is
the act of creating yourself."*
~~Deepak Chopra

PROFITS Affirmation: Today, I ACT to create the "self" I want to become.

POWER Word: ACT

My Affirmation:
___
___

Profitable Trading Wisdom: I ACT to become the "self" I will be for lasting success now. Share 3 goals

___
___
___
___
___
___
___
___
___
___
___
___
___
___
___
___
___

CHALLENGE 23: Grounded Trading GOALS
"The time to begin most things is ten years ago."
~~Mignon McLaughlin

PROFITS Affirmation: I BEGIN to set goals today to build my riches in ten years!

POWER Word: BEGIN

My Affirmation:
_____
_____

Profitable Trading Wisdom: BEGIN to write 10-year goals for yourself.

CHALLENGE 24: Grounded Trading GOALS
"Not a shred of evidence exists in favor of the idea that life is serious."
~~Brenden Gill

PROFITS Affirmation: Life is only as SERIOUS as I make it.

POWER Word: SERIOUS

My Affirmation:
_____
_____

Profitable Trading Wisdom: Recall 5 – 7 "almost" goals that you set for yourself that were not SERIOUS enough, but you never did anything with them.

_____
_____
_____
_____
_____
_____
_____
_____
_____
_____
_____
_____
_____
_____
_____
_____
_____
_____

CHALLENGE 25: Grounded Trading GOALS

*"Life has a way of becoming complicated,
and it is only through
great effort that we can keep it simple."*
~~John C. Maxwell; How Successful People Grow p.57

PROFITS Affirmation: I have discovered how to keep my life SIMPLE for FOREX trading.

POWER Word: SIMPLE

My Affirmation:
_____
_____

Profitable Trading Wisdom: Describe how keeping your life SIMPLE makes your FOREX trading goals SIMPLE.

_____
_____
_____
_____
_____
_____
_____
_____
_____
_____
_____
_____
_____
_____

CHAPTER 4: PROSPERITY TRADING PLAN

*"It takes as much energy to
wish as it does to plan."*
~~Eleanor Roosevelt

A FOREX Prosperity Trading Plan organizes the trader to execute FOREX trading with success based on your Mindset Mastery, market analysis, and personal comforts. When a plan is implemented, it makes trading an easier sequence of events, and reduces the chance of your account being blown. Typically, a plan is in place to keep you on track. It is no different with the FOREX Prosperity Trading Plan. Unless the Prosperity Trading Plan is implemented, it is no good.

A major asset of having a FOREX Prosperity Plan is to fully apply Mindset Mastery to keep the scary thoughts away. Fear of Missing Out (FOMO) is a "Big Boogey Man" thought that causes a trader to sell too soon and hinders trading. Feeling like you are missing out on trades that could make money can cause the trader to irrationally enter or exit trades. This is a sure way to drain your account of hard-earned gains. Market behavior will provide what it provides… the only information it can. It is what it is… So, reduce your stress, control what you can control and follow a trading plan for better health and wealth!

*"You measure the size of the accomplishment by the obstacles
you had to overcome to reach your goals."*
~~Booker T. Washington

It has been said that a FOREX Prosperity Plan is like using a GPS for travel. Moving to a foreign country or even going on a road trip would not be considered these days without using a GPS! There is a level of comfort when you have an idea that the GPS will get you where you want to go. Your FOREX Prosperity Plan can do the same. Your Plan will allow you to trade outside of your comfort zone so you can grow as a trader. It can also allow you to trade outside of a certain comfort zone so you can grow as a trader.

"By failing to prepare, you are preparing to fail."
~~Benjamin Franklin

Think of this document as a fluid, living thing. For example, as your account grows, you will be able to use a higher level of risk with your trades. This should be reflected in your Prosperity Trading Plan.

Just like when using your GPS to go to the grocery store the first time in a new town, your FOREX Prosperity Plan allows you to limit the "wrong turns". You can more easily be redirected to check your Mindset or modify your trades to ensure ongoing profitability to protect your account balance.

Life will bring challenges and possibly changes that will alter your trading experience. Your FOREX Prosperity Plan can be adapted to reflect the changes life brings. As you apply your daily learning of FOREX, new knowledge will allow you to Master your Mindset.

Updating your GPS is a good thing. Updating your "trading GPS" will show you where the new roads are, even if the market has not indicated that those roads are to be taken at the current time.

"There is no telling how many miles you will have to run while chasing a dream."
~~Author Unknown

One of the biggest decisions you will make is to determine what type of FOREX trader you are. This is also the basic structure of your Prosperity Trading Plan. There is a variety of different types of traders and it is up to you to identify the type trader you identify with most closely. Do you like to have all trades closed out in a day like a day trader in, 1 – 4 hours? Do you want a measured number of pips a day like a high maintenance scalper? Maybe you want to leave trades running for weeks or months as long-term traders do? Do you prefer low maintenance swing trading?

No matter what type of trader you are, your Prosperity Plan will help you identify your monetary goals for trading and for life. This includes how much you plan to reasonably invest initially. Take time to save or earn money that you DO NOT mind losing. Losses will be unavoidable. Protecting the funds in your account is most important and will depend on what the markets present to you, your account balance and of course how the markets move for each trade. Do not overleverage yourself. Learn what levels you are comfortable with and manage your risk!

"The secret of getting ahead is getting started."
~~Mark Twain

Another decision that must be made, is which strategy will work best for you. There are almost as many strategies as there are traders. Only you can answer this question based on what type of trader you are and your own personal comfort when trading money that could be lost. Some strategies are dependent on the time frame and must be followed exactly! Plan your trade and Trade your plan! It is up to each one of us as FOREX traders to make prosperity decisions that we can live with, to protect the money in our accounts, and to make it grow. Create your FOREX Prosperity Trading Plan any way you like, just promise yourself you will write something. As time goes on, you will find exactly what works to make your FOREX experience exactly what you need it to be.

FOREX PROSPERITY TRADING PLAN COMPONENTS

A list of FOREX Prosperity Trading Plan Components

Mindset Mastery

WHY

Motivation

Strengths & Weaknesses

Type of Trader

Structure

Sensible Budget/Monetary Goals

Education/Research

Strategy

Fundamentals/Technical Tools

Watch List

Reasonable Initial Investment/Account Balance

Responsible Risk Management

Timing of the Market/Price Action

Exit/Escape Indexes

CELEBRATION

"A step towards what you FEAR is a mile towards MASTERING it."
~~Matshona Dhlywayo

Genie Craff

MY PROSPERITY TRADING PLAN

Today's Date: _____ Evaluation Date: _____

1. I Master my Mindset for FOREX when I:
   _____
   _____

2. My Motivation comes from my Strengths and Weaknesses…
   _____
   _____

3. I am the following Type of Trader and I use the following Strategy, because…
   _____
   _____

4. My Education/Research has taught me…
   _____
   _____

5. My Account Balance is: _____
   My Monetary GOAL: _____

6. Based on my Account Balance, my Responsible Risk Management is: _____

7. My Entry Indicators are:
   _____
   _____

8. My Exit Indicators are:
   _____
   _____

9. I will start (add a component):
   _____

10. I will keep (a component):
    _____

11. I will stop (remove a component):
    _____

EXECUTING ENRICHING FOREX PROSPERITY PLAN EVALUATIONS

Completing regular evaluations of your FOREX Prosperity Trading Plan provides you with tremendous insight and information. Evaluation provides information and builds confidence. Consider the following every three months:

Today's date: _____

1. How am I Mastering my Mindset for FOREX?
   _____
   _____
   _____
   _____

2. Based on my trading strategy, what needs to change with my Prosperity Trading Plan?
   _____
   _____
   _____
   _____

3. How has my account balance changed? What is working? What is not?
   _____
   _____
   _____
   _____

4. How should I change my Responsible Risk Management to be more successful?
   _____
   _____
   _____
   _____

5. How are my Trade Entry and Exit Indicators working to enter and exit trades?
   _____
   _____

6. What part of FOREX do I still need to learn to be more successful?
   _____
   _____
   _____
   _____

7. What are my current questions? Who can I ask for help?
   _____
   _____
   _____
   _____

8. My next Enriching FOREX Prosperity Plan Evaluation will be on this date: _____

9. NOTES:
   _____
   _____
   _____
   _____
   _____
   _____
   _____
   _____
   _____
   _____
   _____

CHALLENGE 26: Prosperity Planning
"Doing more of what doesn't work
won't make it any better."
~~Charles Givens

PROFITS Affirmation: Today, I practice and commit to what WORKS.

POWER Word: WORKS

My Affirmation:
_____
_____

Profitable Trading Wisdom: List what WORKS for me as I plan to trade FOREX.

CHALLENGE 27: Prosperity Planning
*"Every good golfer keeps his left hand
leading the clubhead through impact."*
~~Lee Trevino

PROFITS Affirmation: My Trading Plan is LEADING me as I trade FOREX.

POWER Word: LEADING

My Affirmation:
_____
_____

Profitable Trading Wisdom: How is your FOREX Trading Plan LEADING you?

_____
_____
_____
_____
_____
_____
_____
_____
_____
_____
_____
_____
_____
_____
_____
_____

CHALLENGE 28: Prosperity Planning
"The more I practice... the luckier I get."
~~Gary Player

PROFITS Affirmation: I see how important it is that I PRACTICE FOREX trading with a DEMO account.

POWER Word: PRACTICE

My Affirmation:
_____
_____

Profitable Trading Wisdom: Tally the PRACTICE results of your last 8 FOREX DEMO account trades.

_____
_____
_____
_____
_____
_____
_____
_____
_____
_____
_____
_____
_____
_____
_____
_____
_____
_____

CHALLENGE 29: Prosperity Planning
"Success is the sum of small efforts, repeated,
day in and day out."
~~Robert Collins

PROFITS Affirmation: Today, I see the sum of my small EFFORTS, my success.

POWER Word: EFFORTS

My Affirmation:
_____
_____

Profitable Trading Wisdom: List 6 small EFFORTS that you repeat daily that add to your success.

CHALLENGE 30: Prosperity Planning

*"Don't be discouraged, it isn't like we
lost a ball game
Or something really important."
~~Charlie Brown, It Was A Short Summer, by Charles M. Schulz*

PROFITS Affirmation: I plan my FOREX trades because planning is IMPORTANT.

POWER Word: IMPORTANT

My Affirmation:
_____
_____

Profitable Trading Wisdom: Describe how IMPORTANT planning is to trading FOREX.
_____
_____
_____
_____
_____
_____
_____
_____
_____
_____
_____
_____
_____
_____
_____

CHAPTER 5: UNBREAKABLE TRADING RULES

"He who reigns within himself and rules passions, desires, and fears is more than a king."
~~John Milton

As is stated in Chapter 1, Unbreakable Trading Rules. YES. Unbreakable. This "diamond in your paper bag" will best protect the money in your FOREX funded account. These rules must be so solid, nothing will allow you to enter a trade without them. Ensure you can identify your Unbreakable Trading Rules, can state them and DO NOT enter trades in which the rules may be broken, no matter what!

Unbreakable Trading Rules can be influenced with ongoing educational opportunities or by learning how to read and mark FOREX charts. The charts provide information and indicators for effective and progressively increasing monetary gain. The charts can tell us when trades are advised and when they are ill-advised.

"You have to play by the rules of the game.
And then you have to play better than anyone else."
~~Unknown

The indicators on which you base your FOREX entries, risk management and trade entries and exits must be identified by you, and only you. Reading the messages found on the charts and in the candlesticks can assist you in achieving your dreams and must be considered in your list of Unbreakable Trading Rules.

Knowing the different types of trade orders that can be placed will also help you with information found on the charts. Charts can even help us identify how much of a stop loss to set. These answers should determine your Unbreakable Trading Rules for successful trading.

Your individual comfort zone with your money will be the greatest determining factor. Your Watch List, Responsible Risk Management, Entry and Exit Indicators will all impact your account balance.

"I am FREE because I alone am morally responsible for everything I do."
~~Robert Heinlein

A concept that works well when writing FOREX Unbreakable Trading Rules is called "Black and White Thinking". This concept is used to define ideas for each Rule. Can YOU:

1. Identify a potential rule you are thinking of including in our Unbreakable Trading Rules list?
2. Describe completely what the Unbreakable Rule will look like when included?
3. Anticipate your feelings if you broke your Unbreakable Rules and how it will affect your Mindset if you did?
4. Analyze your actions when following this Rule. Does the Rule serve your intentions?
5. Examine the consequences once you follow the Rule.
6. Can you successfully use the Rule with every trade to meet your Grounded Trading Goals, and Prosperity Trading Plan?

"Either you run the day, or the day runs you."
~~Jim Rohn

A good pilot will not fly into the mountains without having an exact plan as to how to get out, be it to circle or to land. Just like a pilot who does not want to crash, a FOREX trader should make sure they do not get into a trade where there is not a planned solution, in order not to crash. Each trader must find their own comfort zone as to how much they are willing to lose in a trade.

Respected mentors and Brokers may recommend that no more than 10% of the total of the account should be risked or the money could be lost. Remember, if the main purpose of the trader is to protect their bottom line, risking 10% may be too much for YOU. You may ask other traders to provide additional knowledge as to how much of their account is risked on each trade or for their entire trading session. That information again should come from someone you trust. To be safe, try their advice in your DEMO account first. Be a test pilot for your changes. Only you will know for sure.

"Strength does not come from winning.
Your struggles develop your strength.
When you go through hardships and decide not to surrender,
that is strength."
~~Arnold Schwarzenegger

Below are some items to incorporate when setting Unbreakable Trading Rules:

1. Determine your Mindset. If you are distracted or uneasy, don't trade until you can confirm your Mindset is in the right place, no matter how long that may be. Get help if necessary.
2. Review your WHY statement.
3. Implement the Daily Learning information from the last learning session, whether the new knowledge came from personal study, a workshop, training or even a national event or speaker.
4. Identify only High Probability Trades based on the knowledge you have.
5. Verify your Risk to Reward ratio (1:3). 70% is good. 50% is not good.
6. Pinpoint your Trade Entry Indicators.
7. Always use a Stop Loss or include trailing stop orders.
8. Establish the Trade Exit Indicators.
9. Journal each trade.
10. Evaluate each trade completely for what worked whether DEMO or real.
11. Make notes on what to learn next.

> *"Happiness is when what you think, what you say,
> and what you do are in harmony."*
> ~~Mahatma Gandhi

When your Unbreakable Trading Rules are crystal clear, you will see them unfolding in the dark of night. You will soon not have to review them as closely. Belief drives rules and planned actions so deeply that it can be breathed in like fog. Cool, moist and mostly invisible when you get up close. You will be out of the storm of confusion and into the sunny awareness of practice and experience with FOREX trading.

Some have found that incorporating much of what has been written in this book so far into a checklist is the easiest way to implement and use all this information. The following is a checklist format. Use this to enhance your trading experience.

MY UNBREAKABLE TRADING RULES CHECKLIST

I, _____, will only trade FOREX when the following is in place.

1. My Mindset must be

   _____
   _____
   _____
   _____

   before I trade.
2. _____ I confirm I have reviewed my WHY statement and my Grounded Goals.
3. I will implement

   _____
   _____
   _____
   _____

   which I learned during my last training session.
4. I identify my High Probability Trades, using the tools listed, by this criteria:

   _____
   _____
   _____

5. My Risk to Reward Ratio is: _____
6. I pinpoint my Trade Entry Indicators. They are:

   _____
   _____
   _____
   _____

7. The Order Types I will use are:

   _____
   _____
   _____

8. I will use these Stop Loss points or a Trailing Stop Loss that looks like this:

   _____
   _____
   _____

9. I establish my Trade Exit Indicators. They are:

   _____
   _____
   _____

10. _____ I Journaled each trade today.
11. _____ I evaluated each trade.
12. What Worked:

    _____
    _____
    _____
    _____

13. What didn't Work:

    _____
    _____
    _____
    _____

14. My questions and notes for what to learn next:

    _____
    _____
    _____
    _____
    _____

CHALLENGE 31: Unbreakable Trading Rules
"The only place where success comes before work is in the dictionary."
~~Vidal Sassoon

PROFITS Affirmation: Today, I WORK on my unbreakable trading rules for FOREX trading.

POWER Word: WORK

My Affirmation:
___

Profitable Trading Wisdom: Use this space to WORK on your unbreakable trading rules for FOREX.
___

CHALLENGE 32: *Unbreakable Trading Rules*
"Rules are not necessarily sacred,
principles are."
~~Franklin D. Roosevelt

PROFITS Affirmation: I learn unbreakable FOREX trading RULES to play better than anyone else.

POWER Word: RULES

My Affirmation:

_____
_____

Profitable Trading Wisdom: How does your unbreakable FOREX trading RULES assist you to play better than anyone else?

_____
_____
_____
_____
_____
_____
_____
_____
_____
_____
_____
_____
_____
_____

CHALLENGE 33: Unbreakable Trading Rules
"The young (wo)man knows the rules.
The old (wo)man knows the exceptions."
~~Oliver Wendell Holmes, Sr.

PROFITS Affirmation: There are no EXCEPTIONS to my unbreakable FOREX trading rules.

POWER Word: EXCEPTIONS

My Affirmation:
_____
_____

Profitable Trading Wisdom: Provide 3 reasons why there should be no EXCEPTIONS to your FOREX trading rules.

_____
_____
_____
_____
_____
_____
_____
_____
_____
_____
_____
_____
_____
_____
_____
_____

CHALLENGE 34: Unbreakable Trading Rules
"I follow three rules: Do the right thing, do the best you can, and always show people you care."
~~Lou Holtz

PROFITS Affirmation: I show people I CARE.

POWER Word: CARE

My Affirmation:
_____
_____

Profitable Trading Wisdom: I show people I CARE with the following unbreakable FOREX trading rule.

CHALLENGE 35: Unbreakable Trading Rules
"Bend the rules only if you have learned them.
Break the rules only if you have mastered them."
~~Matshona Dhliwayo

PROFITS Affirmation: I have my MASTERED my unbreakable FOREX trading rules.

POWER Word: MASTERED

My Affirmation:
_____
_____

Profitable Trading Wisdom: Contemplate how you have MASTERED your unbreakable FOREX trading rules.

CHAPTER 6: TRADE ENTRY AND EXIT INDICATORS

"The price of anything is the amount of life you exchange for it."
~~Henry David Thoreau

Making decisions has a great deal to do with the execution of your Trading Prosperity Plan. Some people are unable to "let a trade fly" because there are too many decisions to make when deciding to enter high probability trades.

Both internal and external factors make up the trading environment as it pertains to FOREX trading. Internal factors include your beliefs, WHY, personal biases, restrictions and experience. External factors include your availability to obtain the cost of and the availability of FOREX education, for you, your family, and maybe your friends.

**Internal Factors + External Factors =
Trading Environment**

Your trading choices are greatly impacted by your personal comfort level. Your personal comfort is made up of your values, your comfort and relationship to money. To make confident decisions when placing a trade, it is important to understand what market price is telling you.

Those who seek exact entries can be overwhelmed. All that can be learned in your own personal study, or through a mentor or program is important. Come to rely on what you have learned about price action, timing, entry, and other factors yourself.

**Trading Environment + Personal Comfort =
Better Entry and Exit Choices**

---

*"I am not a product of my circumstances.
I am a product of my decisions."*
~~John Milton

Mindset Mastery is the first component and will provide you with the greatest amount of comfort as you decide on entries and exits. Being fearful about a trade does not set the correct framework to be a successful trader. Building your confidence is up to you. The higher your confidence level, the more focus you can devote to trading.

Your Daily Learning Skills application is the second component. This is one certain thing in FOREX trading that can be controlled by you. It will also can help you to get comfortable determining when to enter any trade. Vocabulary and terminology are important when you are communicating or trading with other traders.

The third component of Entry and Exit Indicators is the system you choose. FOREX systems can be as different as the Apple computer is to a PC. Some basics are the same, but overall, there also are many differences. Aim to choose a system you can successfully implement daily. Give any system enough time to wash out any "newbie" error. Test it thoroughly, then decide if the effort to completely change systems is worth the effort. It may be.

Next, the system will have new procedures of its own. The system may dictate that you should enter trades when a certain pattern of candlesticks is present. Other systems may suggest that trades are entered when shapes are drawn on a chart. No matter what system you have chosen, it is very important to follow the exact rules as dictated by that system. Mixing systems is not recommended and could cost you your account balance.

"The best way to predict the future is to create it."
~~Unknown

Last, ensure that your strategy has consistent methods. One consistent that you can control is that you study only one pair for a considerable length of time. By doing this, you will have a better sense of when the market pivots or reverses. Know how fast or slow your pair produces pips to help you make profitable trading choices.

Many traders use their Unbreakable Trading Rules as a "checklist" to identify their analysis tools, entry and exit strategies, risk to reward, and the percentage of risk for all trading positions entered at the same time. This will also help to protect the hard-earned money in your account. If these terms are unfamiliar, it is time to find out what they mean and how they impact trading and your bottom line.

If you choose, create your personalized Unbreakable Trading Rules as a checklist in order to ensure your trading experience is all that you want it to be. Daily participation in this educational process better protects a trader from online trading with inaccurate information, suffering account losses and unnecessary frustration. Increasingly successful trades will build confidence and provide valuable information to repeat as they trade in the future and may provide tips to share with other traders.

"The great aim of education is not knowledge but action,"
~~Herbert Spencer

CHALLENGE 36: Trade Entry Indicators
"Inability to make decisions is one of the
principle reasons executives fail."
~~John C. Maxwell

PROFITS Affirmation: As PRINCIPLE, I make appropriate FOREX trading decisions.

POWER Word: PRINCIPLE

My Affirmation:
_____
_____

Profitable Trading Wisdom: Which PRINCIPLE allows you to make appropriate FOREX trading decisions?

_____
_____
_____
_____
_____
_____
_____
_____
_____
_____
_____
_____
_____
_____
_____
_____

CHALLENGE 37: Trade Entry Indicators
"Do not wait; the time will never be 'just right'.
Start where you stand, and work with whatever
tools you may have at your command,
and better tools will be found as you go along."
~~George Herbert

PROFITS Affirmation: I work well with the TOOLS I have.

POWER Word: TOOLS

My Affirmation:
_____
_____

Profitable Trading Wisdom: List 3 tools that you have now and 5 tools you believe you will need as you go along.

CHALLENGE 38: Trade Entry Indicators

"As long as you're being honest and there's intention in what you are doing, then I think that energy permeates your field and becomes like a homing signal for other people with like energies."

~~SZA

PROFITS Affirmation: I am honest and have INTENTION, so energy permeates my field.

POWER Word: INTENTION

My Affirmation:
_____
_____

Profitable Trading Wisdom: Share how INTENTION signals your energy with FOREX trading.

_____
_____
_____
_____
_____
_____
_____
_____
_____
_____
_____
_____
_____
_____
_____

CHALLENGE 39: Trade Entry Indicators
"I have learned that as long as I hold fast to my
beliefs and values, and follow my own moral compass,
then the only expectations I need to live up to
are my own."
~~First Lady, Dr. Michelle Obama

PROFITS Affirmation: I live up to my own EXPECTATIONS.

POWER Word: EXPECTATIONS

My Affirmation:
_____
_____

Profitable Trading Wisdom: Share how your beliefs, values and moral compass formed your EXPECTATIONS for your trade entry indicators.

_____
_____
_____
_____
_____
_____
_____
_____
_____
_____
_____
_____
_____
_____
_____

CHALLENGE 40: Trade Entry Indicators
*"In formal logic, a contradiction is the
signal of defeat,
but in the evolution of real knowledge it
marks the first step
in progress toward a victory."
~~Alfred North Whitehead*

PROFITS Affirmation: Real knowledge marks the first step in progress towards my VICTORY.

POWER Word: VICTORY

My Affirmation:
_____
_____

Profitable Trading Wisdom: What 5 items of real knowledge mark your progress towards your FOREX VICTORY?
_____
_____
_____
_____
_____
_____
_____
_____
_____
_____
_____
_____
_____
_____
_____
_____

CHAPTER 7: FOREX EDUCATION ~ INCORPORATING DAILY LEARNING

"Believe you can and you are halfway there."
~~Theodore Roosevelt

What is the best way to learn about FOREX trading? FOREX trading is the active buying or selling of foreign currencies. The foreign exchange market determines the foreign exchange rate. All aspects of buying, selling, and exchanging currencies are determined in this market.

FOREX traders include banks, central banks, corporations, institutional investors and individual traders. Markets are balanced and, international trade and tourism are all facilitated by FOREX trading. Most individuals trade simply to make a profit. They do this by learning how to trade in the FOREX market on their own. Increasing successful trades will build confidence and provide information to share with other traders.

FOREX education can be found in a variety of places, mostly online. There are many companies which offer this training. Research all you can about any company you decide to engage in for your educational experience. As always, cost will be a consideration. Make sure you understand all costs up front and what materials you will need before starting.

"...The way we react to things is a big indicator of our character and what type of person we are."
~~Zendaya

Reading reviews online can be helpful, but the most reliable critiques come from speaking to others who have made the decision to learn from the company you are interested in. Do they have poor reviews or regrets from those who have chosen the same company? What would they have changed?

Determine ways to "get your head in the game" or "mindset mastery" BEFORE you begin to trade. Daily offerings for your participation during your educational process will keep a trader on track and from online trading frustration. Your success will depend on how you have mastered your mindset, your knowledge of the FOREX marketplace, and the pair groups. For FOREX trading to be fully successful for you, put in time and preparation.

"Many people love the idea of you, but lack the maturity to handle the reality of you as a successful FOREX trader."
~Genie Craff

Practicing a routine of Daily Learning prevents procrastination. Procrastinating learning more about market movement and price action will halt the progress of your trading skills. Lessons learned from the tasks that you outlined in the last trading session will soon be lost if not applied immediately. Putting off a training session that you can still do today, means forgoing information that could have helped you in your next trade tomorrow. Do this for a year and you'll be putting yourself behind those you see becoming successful traders.

Your financial success will depend on your knowledge and preparation for FOREX trading. To join the 5% of successful FOREX traders, spend time learning FOREX trading skills. This could be training found in a college course, back office, watching videos, live webinars in an online setting, or even a casual conversation with another trader. Determine ways to "get your head in the game" or your Mindset Mastered long before you begin to trade. Learn one more thing to improve your trading experience today, and be assured it will impact your next trade, in the next week, next month, and the years ahead.

Learn why it is better to focus on the higher time frames, or other skills which may have allowed you to miss what price action was telling you in your early trading experiences. Find examples of what worked for you in your Demo account. This belief builds consistent confidence in learning and trading.

Become your best "self" in your trading journey, by being yourself, and taking responsibility for yourself. So, what does it take to be your best? Take responsibility and ask questions of your mentor or of your broker to help you when stumped. Ask for help. As adults we don't like to admit that we might need help to show us the way. Trying to find your way to the best trading situations without knowing the way is no different than an ill-advised trip to the beach in the high winds of a hurricane. It could be very expensive and scary.

"If you take responsibility for yourself
you will develop a hunger
to accomplish your dreams."
~~Les Brown

CHALLENGE 41: Daily Learning/Education

*"Leadership and learning are
indispensable to each other."*
~~John F. Kennedy

PROFITS Affirmation: I am LEARNING something new about FOREX trading every day.

POWER Word: LEARNING

My Affirmation:
_____
_____

Profitable Trading Wisdom: How has LEARNING become leadership in your experience?

_____
_____
_____
_____
_____
_____
_____
_____
_____
_____
_____
_____
_____
_____
_____

CHALLENGE 42: Daily Learning/Education

"Anytime you learn something new, there's going to be a point of resistance. Here's what that means; you're growing."
~~John Assaraf

PROFITS Affirmation: I accept points of RESISTANCE as growth.

POWER Word: RESISTANCE

My Affirmation:
_____
_____

Profitable Trading Wisdom: List 5 "stand out" educational experiences or trainings that have felt like RESISTANCE but expanded your trading skills!

_____
_____
_____
_____
_____
_____
_____
_____
_____
_____
_____
_____
_____
_____
_____

CHALLENGE 43: Daily Learning/Education
"I play to win. Whether in practice or a real game."
~~Michael Jordan

PROFITS Affirmation: I PLAY to win.

POWER Word: PLAY

My Affirmation:
_____
_____

Profitable Trading Wisdom: I PLAY to win. Write down 4 Rules to enter a FOREX trade and 4 Rules to exit a FOREX trade.

CHALLENGE 44: Daily Learning/Education
"A good leader encourages followers to tell him what he needs to know, not what he wants to hear."
~~John C. Maxwell

PROFITS Affirmation: To connect with others, I use active listening to learn their NEEDS.

POWER Word: NEEDS

My Affirmation:
___
___

Profitable Trading Wisdom: Write what active listening means to you and how do you know you are practicing great listening to learn their NEEDS?

___
___
___
___
___
___
___
___
___
___
___
___
___
___
___
___
___

CHALLENGE 45: *Daily Learning/Education*
*"It's what you learn after you
know it all that counts."*
~~John Wooden, Hall of Fame Basketball Coach

PROFITS Affirmation: I know a lot about FOREX trading, what COUNTS is still coming.

POWER Word: COUNTS

My Affirmation:
_____
_____

Profitable Trading Wisdom: List the last 6 things you have learned about FOREX trading in preparation for what you will learn which is all that COUNTS.

_____
_____
_____
_____
_____
_____
_____
_____
_____
_____
_____
_____
_____
_____
_____
_____
_____
_____

CHAPTER 8: PASSION AND GREED

*"But if you have a passion,
an honest passion, just do it."*
~~Mario Andretti

What is your passion and is it unmatched by about most everything else? Is your passion just to make a huge pile of money? Or is your passion for trading founded in generating unbreakable rules which follow specific entry indicators before a trade is ever entered? This is the passion of the most successful traders. These feelings of expectation that are experienced prior to placing the trade are greatly determined by a Mastered Mindset.

You have heard the saying, "The trend is your friend.". Realizing the power of a trend and following it will increase your passion and success with low-risk profitable trades. However, this is where words of caution are necessary.

Remember, successful trading always begins with Mindset Mastery. Take time to discover and review your Prosperity Trading Plan to keep on track. When it feels like you've already realized (and spent) the profits before you begin or before you exit your plan for trading, you could be in trouble.

*"Everything you ever wanted is
on the other side of fear."*
~~George Adair

Passion and GREED are brothers who play well when only one is winning and is much stronger. Mindset Mastery is found when you know your passion for trading does not turn into GREED. You must be able to leave a trade on the table. Do not focus on making up money lost in consolidation or pullback. Celebrate your trading success. Celebrate others trading practice, success and journey.

Passion is the fire in Mindset Mastery! Passion can most easily be seen in a dream board. Dream boards are not just a fad. They are the joining of passion and vision to make dreams become real. Cutting out pictures of the yachts, mansions, expensive sports cars, island vacations, trips abroad, and other desired thoughts and ideas could be realized into images.

Your dreams are captured within the shiny depictions of images. The most powerful dream boards encompass and capture a dream that is bigger than you! When your financial gain is more than some third world countries entire budget, what do you plan to do to change and improve the lives of others? These ideas too, are loaded onto colorful boards, placed above desks, or on refrigerators, or wherever they will be seen at least seven times a day. What will be your LEGACY?

"I would rather die of PASSION than of boredom."
~~Vincent van Gogh

Personal GREED is displayed by misusing the suggestions of risk management and or a desperation to get money back that was lost during trading or in trying to get rich quick. Only by following your Prosperity Trading Plan to the letter, can you expect to take your profits when they are at their highest, minimalize your losses, but most importantly to protect the money you have in your account.

Even the BEST analysis can be imperfect and can take hard earned profits away. Stay vigilant and aware of your goals. Once you have met your goals for the day, STOP TRADING!

There are 3 types of Trader's greed. The first type mainly develops from a lack of knowledge. This type of greed comes in not fully understanding the levels of risk management and the risk to reward on a single trade or on a group of trades. This the type of greed which is most warned about but not followed until a real account is blown. Sadly, the main responsibility of protecting and maintaining the money invested and earned was not realized.

The second type of trader's GREED comes from winning a series of trades in a row and placing too many positions for additional trades. For example, if two trades were placed and completed in the blue, with positive outcomes, you may think that the pair you have chosen will continue to have similar success.

How do you know this? Market price action is never predictable. Those who study the markets MAY have an idea. They can still be incorrect. Newer traders are most likely to fall into either or both, of these first two phases. Stay vigilant and know your WHY. Remember FOREX is not a quick way to get rich!

"We are in danger of destroying ourselves by our greed and stupidity."
~~Stephen Hawking

The last type of trader's greed can happen to any trader. Newer traders have shared with me that it is very tempting when it seems like the "money is right there… they can see it" to disregard all learning, knowledge, and reason. Often this is because the trader has not identified their "WHY". Then they blow their trading account, and for some, cannot trade until they save again to refund it. Using a DEMO account can allow you to continue to trade while you are rebuilding your real account.

Traders GREED has also been described to me as the feeling that makes a trader hold on way too long to a losing trade. Setting appropriate stop losses can help this, however, when learning, that may be more difficult. When the trader enters out of GREED, or panic from Fear of Missing Out (FOMO) then the market rises to resistance, as it falls, the trader "jumps" out of the trade from panic or fear. Fear makes the trader get out too soon. When the trader jumps from panic or fear, money will be lost.

Those who believe they can "beat the odds" or who get a thrill when trading will fail. You should plan for your account to have both ups and downs. This is not referring to price action going up or down. This is referring to the fact that the balance the trader is supposed to protect, will most likely experience both gains and losses.

Avoid these five blunders which cause stress and cost you money.

1. Do not have unreal expectations. The market is ALWAYS right!
2. Do not try to predict news events which will impact price action.
3. Do not try to trade immediately after the news. The market can be fickle and take a while to settle back in.
4. Do not risk more than your account can handle. From 1% to 10% depending on the balance in your account.
5. Bad trades should be exited quickly. No need to hold on and hope for a change. GET OUT.

> *"You have not lived today until you do
> something for someone who can
> never repay you."*
> ~~John Bunyan

CHALLENGE 46: PASSION

"With the new day comes new strength and new thoughts."
~~Eleanor Roosevelt

PROFITS Affirmation: Each new day brings new STRENGTH.

POWER Word: STRENGTH

My Affirmation:
_____
_____

Profitable Trading Wisdom: List 10 things which bring you STRENGTH.

CHALLENGE 47: PASSION

"You have to be burning with an idea, or a problem, or a wrong that you want to right. If you are not passionate enough from the start, you'll never stick it out."
~~Steve Jobs

PROFITS Affirmation: I am PASSIONATE about FOREX trading.

POWER Word: PASSIONATE

My Affirmation:
_____
_____

Profitable Trading Wisdom: Write how you became PASSIONATE about trading FOREX.

CHALLENGE 48: PASSION

"I have always believed the greater danger is not in aiming too high, but too low, settling for a bogey rather than shooting for an eagle."
~~Peter Scott

PROFITS Affirmation: I aim high on purpose, not SETTLING for playing small.

POWER Word: SETTLING

My Affirmation:
_____
_____

Profitable Trading Wisdom: In not SETTLING, how do you aim high?

CHALLENGE 49: PASSION
"If passion drives you, let reason hold the reins."
~~Benjamin Franklin

PROFITS Affirmation: I let REASON hold the reins in all my FOREX trading decisions.

POWER Word: REASON

My Affirmation:
___
___

Profitable Trading Wisdom: Jot down the evidence (10) when REASON holds the reins in my FOREX decisions.

CHALLENGE 50: PASSION

"Nothing is as important as passion.
NO matter what
You do with your life, be passionate."
~~Jon Bon Jovi

PROFITS Affirmation: I am passionate about all aspects of my LIFE.

POWER Word: LIFE

My Affirmation:
___
___

Profitable Trading Wisdom: List 10 things you are passionate about your LIFE, outside of FOREX.

CHALLENGE 51: GREED

"I owe my success to having listened respectfully to the very best advice, and then going away and doing the exact opposite."
~~G. K. Chesterton

PROFITS Affirmation: I have LISTENED respectfully to the very best advice for FOREX trading.

POWER Word: LISTENED

My Affirmation:
_____
_____

Profitable Trading Wisdom: Share 2 experiences about LISTENING to great advice about FOREX trading.

CHALLENGE 52: GREED
"Don't look where you fell, but where you slipped."
~~African Proverb

PROFITS Affirmation: I protect the money in my FOREX trading live account and take note if I SLIPPED.

POWER Word: SLIPPED

My Affirmation:
_____
_____

Profitable Trading Wisdom: Share what a proper FOREX trade means to you? What does it look like when you have SLIPPED?

_____
_____
_____
_____
_____
_____
_____
_____
_____
_____
_____
_____
_____
_____
_____
_____
_____

CHALLENGE 53: GREED
"If things go wrong... don't go with them."
~~Roger Babson

PROFITS Affirmation: I contain my emotions when a FOREX trade is going WRONG.

POWER Word: WRONG

My Affirmation:
_____
_____

Profitable Trading Wisdom: What do you do to contain your emotions when a trade is going WRONG?

_____
_____
_____
_____
_____
_____
_____
_____
_____
_____
_____
_____
_____
_____
_____
_____
_____

CHALLENGE 54: GREED
"Experience is a terrible teacher
who sends horrific bills."
~~Anonymous

PROFITS Affirmation: I learn something new and I am gaining EXPERIENCE with each trade.

POWER Word: EXPERIENCE

My Affirmation:
___
___

Profitable Trading Wisdom: Gaining EXPERIENCE in FOREX trading can be expensive. List as many tips as you can remember to keep your "EXPERIENCE" from becoming expensive.

___
___
___
___
___
___
___
___
___
___
___
___
___
___

CHALLENGE 55: GREED
"Try not to worry... take each day just one anxiety attack at a time."
~~Tom Wilson

PROFITS Affirmation: I work to protect the money I have in my trading account and to reduce my ANXIETY.

POWER Word: ANXIETY

My Affirmation:
___
___

Profitable Trading Wisdom: How do you use proper Risk Management to reduce ANXIETY and protect the money in your FOREX live trading account?

___
___
___
___
___
___
___
___
___
___
___
___
___
___
___
___

CHAPTER 9: RESPONSIBLE RISK MANAGEMENT

*"I can't change the direction of the wind, but
I can adjust my sails to
always reach my destination."*
~~Jimmy Dean

Just as you cannot change the direction of the wind, you cannot change the direction of a trade. The market will move as it may. Because every second of the market is based on supply and demand, it is important to understand what that means. Supply is the quantity of the money that can be sold at various prices, (i.e. traded). It is the same for commodities like oil and gold. Demand is how much someone will pay for it, or in our case how much we are willing to trade for it. The market will give what it gives. Price action is a kite in the wind. It is always correct, no matter what moves it makes.

So how does this relate to appropriate FOREX risk management? Appropriate risk management should occur BEFORE a trade is placed. The market provides all the clues to assist those who create trading strategy or to show an individual trader a high probability trade. The candlesticks each carry information, some indicate reversal and others indicate consolidation, expansion or retracement. These messages allow the trader to determine what level of risk management is appropriate for their trades.

"Enjoy when you can and endure when you must."
~~Johann Wolfgang Goethe

The lack of understanding appropriate risk management can come with a cost. Every trade that is entered will require a lot size (or risk) when converted to dollars, that you are personally comfortable losing. This is based on the pips. A pip is the movement found in the fourth decimal of the exchange rate. Pips are how trades are measured. Pips are divided into MICRO LOTS, MINI LOTS, and STANDARD LOTS to create the lot size (or risk).

It looks like this:

Exchange rate for EURUSD	1.1234 + 2 pips	= 1.1236
MICRO LOT	.01 -.09	$.10 cents to $.90 cents per PIP
MINI LOT	.1 - .9	$1 to $9 per PIP
STANDARD LOT	1.00	$10 per PIP

As a general guideline, it is not wise to risk high lot sizes with a relatively low account balance. You will risk blowing your account and potentially losing all the money in your account, whether you have made gains or simply just added funds. Practice appropriate risk management. This is crucial.

"Defeat is simply a signal to press onward."
~~Helen Keller

You can, however, take responsibility for what you do when FOREX trading. Taking responsibility is not always easy. Take responsibility and own up to the fact that you may have read an indicator incorrectly. You must take responsibility for placing incorrect information into a trade or setting a stop loss that is too tight. Take responsibility for your own lousy risk management. Take responsibility for both the losses and the gains. By taking responsibility for your actions in trades, you will grow as a trader and the experiences are valuable learning opportunities.

In your childhood, there were parental figures who insisted on you taking responsibility. Now as a FOREX trader you may have only yourself or those you love. It is important to take a moment here to reflect on what the impact of taking responsibility for your full trading experience may have on those who love you. This can impact many other aspects of your life, so take the time needed to ensure that your description of your experience, your personal FOREX trading story matches your expectations, your vision, dreams and your bank account.

"The easiest path is the least rewarding."
~~Genie Craff

Albert Einstein knew that compound interest would multiply anything it is applied to, including your bank account, faster than any other factor. It is the most powerful force in the universe. Now it is in your hands and can be used with FOREX trading. Compound interest is interest that is calculated on initial principal, which also includes the accumulated amounts of previous periods, in this case for a series of trades.

How does compound interest work? Compound interest pays interest on a specific amount of money, over a specified period. Each time a new amount is attained, interest will be made on the total of those amounts. It is paid to you, when it is added to your total. I.e. For each $100 in your account, that doubled every month for one year, the new total is $204,800.

Compound interest is much like putting off one more thing that you can still do today, every day for a year. Identify that one last thing to help your mindset today and it will impact your tomorrows, your weeks, and your months, in the years ahead. Earn 2.5% a day and the extra is icing on the cake of life! What do you know about compounding interest now? How it will impact your life in a week, a month, 6 months, a year, 2 years and 5 years?

"Time is your friend and impulse is your enemy.
Take advantage of compound interest and don't let be
captivated by the siren song of the market."
~~Warren Buffet

FOREX RISK MANAGEMENT CHARTS

The following is a guide for Risk Management. Most successful traders risk no more than 2% of their account per day for each trade and 5% per day overall. Some newer traders shared that these levels were way too high with a new account with less than $1000. The decision is up to you!

$100	.01 - .02
$200 - $300	.02 - .04
$400 - $500	.04 - .06
$600 - $700	.06 - .08
$800 - $900	.08 - 1.00
$1000 - $2000	.10 - .15
$3000 - $4000	.30 - .35
$5000 – 6,000	.50 - .55
$7000 - $8000	.70 - .75
$8000 - $10000	.90 – 1.0

"Motivation is the art of getting people to do what you want them to do because they want to do it."
~~Dwight D. Eisenhower

CHALLENGE 56: Responsible Risk Management
*"I've failed over and over in my life.
And that is why I succeed."*
~~Michael Jordan

PROFITS Affirmation: I SUCCEED when I fail over and over.

POWER Word: SUCCEED

My Affirmation:
_____
_____

Profitable Trading Wisdom: Here I listed 7 things that I failed over and over to SUCCEED.

_____
_____
_____
_____
_____
_____
_____
_____
_____
_____
_____
_____
_____
_____
_____
_____
_____
_____
_____
_____

CHALLENGE 57: Responsible Risk Management
"Education costs money, but then so does ignorance."
~~Sir Claus Mosir

PROFITS Affirmation: Today, I claim IGNORANCE costs more than education; I get the education I need.

POWER Word: IGNORANCE

My Affirmation:
_____
_____

Profitable Trading Wisdom: IGNORANCE about risk management cost me... Describe and be specific.

_____
_____
_____
_____
_____
_____
_____
_____
_____
_____
_____
_____
_____
_____
_____
_____
_____

CHALLENGE 58: Responsible Risk Management
"What is measured improves."
~~Peter F. Drucker

PROFITS Affirmation: I MEASURE my risk to manage my lot size before I trade.

POWER Word: MEASURE

My Affirmation:
___

Profitable Trading Wisdom: Listed are 10 ways I MEASURE how I am a better person when FOREX trading.

CHALLENGE 59: Responsible Risk Management
"There is no telling how many miles you will have to run while chasing a dream."
~~Author Unknown

PROFITS Affirmation: I will run every mile necessary while CHASING my dream.

POWER Word: CHASING

My Affirmation:
_____
_____

Profitable Trading Wisdom: Responsible Risk Management is a part of CHASING my dream because:

_____
_____
_____
_____
_____
_____
_____
_____
_____
_____
_____
_____
_____
_____
_____
_____

CHALLENGE 60: Responsible Risk Management
"Not everything that is faced can be changed,
but nothing ever can be changed until it is faced."
~~James Baldwin

PROFITS Affirmation: I face everything that needs to be FACED.

POWER Word: FACED

My Affirmation:
_____
_____

Profitable Trading Wisdom: The last 4 things I FACED about my FOREX risk management made me more responsible. They are:

_____
_____
_____
_____
_____
_____
_____
_____
_____
_____
_____
_____
_____
_____
_____
_____
_____
_____
_____

CHAPTER 10: WOMEN IN FOREX (FOR YOUR EYES ONLY)

*"All women, everywhere, have the same hopes:
We want to be self-sufficient and create
better lives for ourselves and our loved ones."*
~~Melinda Gates

FINANCIAL FACTS:
- 70 MILLION women control 7 TRILLION in purchasing power
- Mothers are responsible for the financial education for children
- Women traditionally invest and save more conservatively than men
- Women lag significantly behind men in retirement planning
- 71% of women over 65 have no pensions
- Only 10% of women retire with a retirement plan.
- Average income of women over 65 is $12,000 per YEAR
- 3 in 10 non-married women 65+ are poor or near poor

The above facts are shocking and VERY REAL. These numbers must be turned around so our mothers, aunts, sisters and daughters will not fall into the claws of these statistics. Getting a solid financial education is probably the most significant factor to change these numbers. No, FOREX is not for everyone.

However, for some the educational platforms that teach FOREX trading provide far more education than just how to place a trade. If not, then add FOREX financial education to your schedule at least six times a year.

*"I felt most proud on the
success of the Apollo mission."*
~~Katherine Johnson

Successful trading starts with the proper mindset just like anything a woman puts her mind to. Using a trading journal which measures the actual measurable results of each trade allows a woman to confirm what works BEST. Did you like the twin trades when they were successful? Why? Why not just double your risk percentage. These questions make up both the activity of trading and the building of your Mindset Mastery. Take the time needed to keep your Prosperity Plan on track and to ensure you are successfully following your plan as you planned it.

So, are you afraid to Master your Mindset in order to trade more successfully? Is this something you've never done before? Sometimes, for women, the fear of being successful holds us back. What would others think of us, especially if we had already shared with them how prosperous FOREX trading could be, if now when someone asks, you must tell them you are in drawdown or took a loss? What now? Time for more learning!

Mentoring for women may look slightly different than it does for men. Women speak differently to each other and are typically less knowledgeable about how to make money work for them. This is a vital portion of the education women must seek.

Ask those who can provide you ways to learn for yourself. Ensure you are not only asking for short term answers, like where to place a stop loss. Determine your BEST style of trading, learn to mark charts, and or place fibs for yourself! Ask questions of women who open doors to mansions, luxury car(s) and take vacations to the destinations of their dreams. They are there to help you. Together you understand that helping others helps others get them what they want and in turn, you get what you want.

"I am beginning to measure myself in
strength not pounds,
Sometimes in smiles."
~~Laurie Halse Anderson

A woman's prosperity plan must include what you want to accomplish as you trade each day and long term. This plan works in concert with the compound interest chart. However, a prosperity plan is not a schedule. Your schedule is where your trading, assignments, responsibilities and activities are logged to ensure you are on time for the commitments in your life.

Some women may have responsibilities that require more energy and time. Using the daily trading checklist provides for those tasks that you outlined during the last trading session. Then of course, there's always one more thing that MUST be done. Outlining what needs to be done the next day before you leave your trading place will give you the peace to know what to tackle first the next time you come to trade.

As you create your trading schedule, include your training sessions and set the proper alarms to keep you informed about when the trainings begin or when the markets open. Keep your materials organized and close to fresh paper and pencils. The next tidbit could come without any notice in an online session. Be ready. Your schedule should also include when you will be contacting your mentor. Don't forget to set time aside for that special someone, away from both trading and the children. Plan vacations away from trading. Identify times for trading, times for family and times for FUN!

"Champions keep playing until they get it right."
~~Billie Jean King

A woman's relationship to money is very different than it is for men. A woman who has very little financial education may fear how money works and have little knowledge how money can work for them.

Fear is:	**F** = False	or	**F** = Face
	E = Evidence		**E** = Everything
	A = Appearing		**A** = And
	R = Real		**R** = RISE

When false evidence appears real during a trade, you must face everything and rise or money most likely will be lost. Trading may not be recommended for a woman who has very little money.

Trading is not a get rich scheme. Gamblers go to the casino. Ill-advised, unproven trading activities are gambling. Trading is a business. Treating trading like a business and protecting the bottom line will make the profits grow.

Since women have special responsibilities and relationship to money, it is prudent to talk about a special type of personal GREED. Personal GREED is an enigma for women. Shopping your earnings away will not keep you from being a statistic. Trading may seem like the easiest way to get everything you want.

However, that type of thinking may not work for many business ventures and FOREX trading is no exception. Become a saver. Check your spending and define the difference of what you need and what you simply want. Always use savings to pay off the bills before going into debt when possible. Once you have met your goals for the day, STOP TRADING! Give your account a chance to grow at a strong, even pace.

"Always follow your dream. Dream BIG because my whole career, including any of the things I have accomplished,
I never thought in a million years
that I would be here.
So, it just proves that once you put your
mind to something, YOU can do it!
~~Simone Biles, Gold Winning Olympic Gymnast

Once someone has started or expanded their trading journey, all they want is success. No matter what success looks like. Maybe it is just a few PIPs a day gain, or 'baby' profits, or some simply look forward to proudly sharing with others how successful the last trading session went becomes primary. Once you have met your goals for the day, STOP TRADING!

Don't let anything hold you back from the ultimate success you desire. Allow the dreams to live on. Our dreams are created when we see something someone else has, or we hear of something others have done. So, until there's a better picture of the island and the acreage with the infinity pool, redream the dreams, after all they are dreams. Then, change the images as necessary

There are those who know when to work, when to learn, when to trade and even when to play! That one thing… Knowing when to place the profitable trade could pave a parking lot, buy your luxury car or allow you to choose the home with the infinity pool… There are those who see what can be done when the time is right. Place yourself among the most successful traders. They ACT upon knowing when!

7 Distinctions of Extraordinary Women

1. **MASTERED MINDSET:** Emotions Have A Place
2. **INTEGRITY:** Honor Your Word
3. **POWER:** Use Your Power to Help Others
4. **COURAGE:** Acknowledge FEAR
5. **PEACE:** Spread Peace and Joy
6. **CHARISMA:** Bring Other Women Together
7. **INSPIRE:** Share Possibilities to Inspire Other Women

Many people have left money to their children including the Rockefeller or the Vanderbilt families. For some families, it has worked out well. For others not so much. Leaving a child money is a nice thing to do, however, leaving a child an opportunity for advanced education and financial knowledge is by far, the greatest gift you can leave as your legacy. Dream what you want to dream; go where you want to go; be what you want to be, because you only have one life. LIFE is no dress rehearsal.

"Here's to strong women:
May we be them,
May we know them,
May we raise them,"
~~Unknown

CHALLENGE 61: Women IN FOREX
"She believed she could, so she did."
~~Unknown

PROFITS Affirmation: I BELIEVED so I can do.

POWER Word: BELIEVED

My Affirmation:
_____
_____

Profitable Trading Wisdom: The last time I BELIEVED, I found myself doing…

_____
_____
_____
_____
_____
_____
_____
_____
_____
_____
_____
_____
_____
_____
_____
_____
_____
_____

CHALLENGE 62: Women In FOREX
"Success does not motivate me as much as integrity does."
~~Becky Saurbrunn

PROFITS Affirmation: I have INTEGRITY and it motivates me.

POWER Word: INTEGRITY

My Affirmation:
_____
_____

Profitable Trading Wisdom: INTEGRITY motivates me to…

CHALLENGE 63: Women In FOREX
"You had the power all along my dear."
~~Glinda the Good Witch in The Wizard of Oz
(L. Frank Baum)

PROFITS Affirmation: I have POWER.

POWER Word: POWER

My Affirmation:
_____
_____

Profitable Trading Wisdom: I have power all along when...

CHALLENGE 64: Women In FOREX
"Courage is like a muscle. We strengthen it with use."
~~Ruth Gordon

PROFITS Affirmation: I have COURAGE.

POWER Word: COURAGE

My Affirmation:
_____
_____

Profitable Trading Wisdom: I am unstoppable when my COURAGE is…

CHALLENGE 65: Women In FOREX
"Inner peace begins the moment you choose not
to allow another person or
event to control your emotions."
~~Pima Chodron

PROFITS Affirmation: I use PEACE to control my emotions.

POWER Word: PEACE

My Affirmation:
_____
_____

Profitable Trading Wisdom: I use PEACE to control my emotions with FOREX trading when I...

_____
_____
_____
_____
_____
_____
_____
_____
_____
_____
_____
_____
_____
_____
_____
_____

CHALLENGE 66: Women In FOREX
"Lack of charisma can be fatal."
~~Jenny Holzer

PROFITS Affirmation: I have CHARISMA.

POWER Word: CHARISMA

My Affirmation:
_____
_____

Profitable Trading Wisdom: My CHARISMA can be seen when I am FOREX trading when I…

CHALLENGE 67: Women In FOREX
*"Instead of letting your hardships and failures
discourage or exhaust you,
let them inspire you."*
~~Former First Lady, Dr. Michelle Obama

PROFITS Affirmation: I INSPIRE others when I experience hardship and failure.

POWER Word: INSPIRE

My Affirmation:
_____
_____

Profitable Trading Wisdom: When I experience hardships and failures, I let them INSPIRE me to…

_____
_____
_____
_____
_____
_____
_____
_____
_____
_____
_____
_____
_____
_____

CHAPTER 11: VISION, SUCCESS, AND BIG DREAM

*"Whatever the mind of man can conceive
and believe it can achieve."*
~~Napoleon Hill

Vision lives within each of us. Or does it? The main reason a dream is not fulfilled is because there is no vision behind it. I recently saw a trial experiment on the streets of a large American city. People were offered $10,000 for the taking. Most would have thought the givers would be out of money within minutes. This was not the case.

There was only one person who stopped and asked for money. And this poor man simply asked for $.35 for a bus transfer. When he was offered the rest of the ten thousand dollars, he said no thank you and took the $.35 and got on the bus. Obviously, the man and the many who walked away didn't understand what was being offered. Many will walk away from the right opportunity because they fail to visualize how the opportunity will impart light upon their life.

Dreaming of wealth takes on a tangible element when we visualize our future. Closing our eyes, we can incorporate what we want into more than pictures cut from a magazine. Vision is more meaningful when we realize what we need to change and are willing to do to get what we want. Making these changes can take time and energy. This life adventure is so worth it! Take time to visualize only what you want.

"There are two types of people who will tell you that you cannot make a difference in this world: those who are afraid to try and those who are afraid you will succeed."
~~Ray Goforth

Most of us can see the pictures of our dreams. But few are willing to identify what they're willing to give up for what they want, as this is the beginning of the visionary process. So, the vision never actually gains breath and life. Vision may mean giving up a relationship, a friend, a habit or a way of doing something so that you can make way for that which needs to be done to better your Forex trading journey. It may mean changing up those things that will pave the way for things to be done differently in ways not considered before.

Success is grounded in integrity. Some think this idea is outdated, however, the need for integrity in all we do as humans, could never be greater! Trust, respect and dignity are all founded in integrity. Integrity is defined as, the quality of being honest and having strong moral principles. Values and honesty are small things closely linked to integrity. When you do the right thing, all the time, day after day, week after week and year after year, you develop integrity and character.

When your priorities are right, and you have integrity, you will not think of taking a short cut, hurting another's feelings to get something you desire, or claim work that was not completed by you. Do not confuse integrity with reputation. Your reputation reflects your character. All of us have a reputation. Keep your word. Do not promise what you can't deliver. Learn from constructive criticism. Allow integrity to be a part of your success.

"All progress takes place outside of the comfort zone."
~~Michael John Bobak

Success is defined in as many ways as there are people. Success can be identified as something that is accomplished, something gained as in a job or position. Success is backed by belief and fed by ambition. Perspective is all in how we see what is right in front of us. Perspective is seeing what the market has served us. Making the correct decisions about FOREX trading will bring new perspectives about your vision, success and your dreams.

How would you define success? What inspired FOREX trading nuggets have you implemented today that strengthened your mindset? Could it be a 10 PIP trade or a $10 trade? Maybe it is a $100 decision to stay in a trade in the red, at least for now, as your stop loss has not been hit yet? Maybe it means not trading live at all today, because the market signals do not match your Prosperity Trading Plan and entry indicators.

> *"Every great dream begins with a dreamer.*
> *Always remember you have within you*
> *the strength, the patience, and the PASSION*
> *to reach the stars and change the world."*
> *~~Harriet Tubman*

Many can relate to a bank account which has more than three numbers to the left of the first comma. In other words, more than $100,000. Others are not there yet. Success is defined by each of us in a different way. Don't let your stats get away, journal them. They will tell a story of your trading unlike anything else. Learn what compound interest is and apply it to trading. When you are ready of course!

> *"The difference between what we do, and*
> *what we are capable of doing; would*
> *suffice to solve most of the world's problems."*
> *~~Mahandas Gandhi*

To Dream BIG is a separate mindset that may need to be transformed, for those who are not wealthy. The very rich have a completely different mindset than the general population. This is based on personal traits and understanding how they influence your finances and wealth. For example, saving money takes patience.

Once you are satisfied with what you have, you will cease spending money on things that are not essential. Very rich people are very organized and disciplined. Rich people reflect on their past financial decisions, in order to make solid financial decisions in the future. Creativity and curiosity shape their risk-taking decisions. The importance of goal setting, staying out of debt, and working smart are not lost on the rich.

To Dream BIG, means taking action to fulfill your desires! Have you made plans to drive to the mansion, test the car, and find that vacation home or cruise? Look past the doors to see what else is waiting for you there. Waiting for tomorrow may not seem like it will matter. But to realize months later that you are indeed months behind those traders who stayed with their trading goals, rules and plan, day after day will be a great disappointment. They found themselves opening the doors to the mansion, the luxury car and the vacation home on a regular basis! Where did they take the last cruise?

A single trading idea could be the key to unlocking skills you never knew you had. The amount of the money is far less impressive than the knowledge you gained to trade in the blue, independently over and over again. If you do nothing about it, that trade will be lost forever.

Years later, and possibly many dollars later, you may come to understand what the inspired thought could have been, should have been… Well, let's just say, that trade that could have made you millions. The best traders trade on a demo account for as long as a year while they master their skills. Practice trading on demo accounts to build your confidence for trading with real money. DO NOT skip this step.

Where do you want your trading journey to take you? Have you made the decision to take the first step on this FOREX trading journey?

"Travel is fatal to prejudice, bigotry and narrow-mindedness."
~~Mark Twain

Genie Craff

DREAMS...

You are surely wondering what it will take to make your dreams a reality.
You are wondering what price must be paid, what fear must be faced,
what must be risked, and what must be lost.
What it will take, my friend, is no less than all that you have
and all that you are.

It will take your heart to know the cold pain of the water and jump in any way.
And this you must do, not once, but a thousand times.
You must feel the sting of rejection, the harsh reality of your own doubts
and chose to move forward in the face of the heaviest burdens
any person shall ever bear. This immense weight
will be made mostly of your own
doubts about your abilities, your willingness, your desire even. It will be
combined with a terrible exhaustion that I cannot give you the power to know.
And in all of this, there will be a sadness so heavy
you will struggle to lift even one foot.

In these moments you will face the most horrible of choices—
either to watch your most precious dreams, both those you hold dear today,
and any you have in the future, to watch those dreams
all wither and die before you OR, perhaps worse, to go on.

In these moments it will take all you have to go on.
And as surely as the sun rises and sets, if you give your whole heart
to this dreamy madness, you will at moments, laugh at the absurdity of
the whole endeavor. You will question your own sanity and well you should.
For it is a foolhardy thing to gamble all of yourself and all of your heart.

But, it is my greatest wish for you that you should know the exhaustion,
the terror, the madness of such a risk for in that moment you are a
servant to your dreams—and in that,
ALL GREATNESS LIES.

--Unknown

CHALLENGE 68: Vision
"The only reason I would take up jogging
is to hear heavy breathing again."
~~Erma Bombeck

PROFITS Affirmation: I know WHY I succeed... AGAIN and AGAIN.

POWER Word: AGAIN

My Affirmation:
_____
_____

Profitable Trading Wisdom: List the 10 things that you will do over and over AGAIN as you FOREX trade.

_____
_____
_____
_____
_____
_____
_____
_____
_____
_____
_____
_____
_____
_____
_____
_____
_____
_____

CHALLENGE 69: Vision
"The realities of the world seldom measure up to the
sublime ideas of the human imagination."
~~Bryant H. McGill

PROFITS Affirmation: I use my IMAGINATION to create sublime ideas.

POWER Word: IMAGINATION

My Affirmation:
_____
_____

Profitable Trading Wisdom: Comment how you use your IMAGINATION to create sublime ideas.

CHALLENGE 70: Vision
"Every strike brings me closer
to the next home run."
~~Babe Ruth

PROFITS Affirmation: I visualize every FOREX trade to bring me CLOSER to success.

POWER Word: CLOSER

My Affirmation:
_____
_____

Profitable Trading Wisdom: What Unbreakable Rules do you visualize to ensure your trades will bring you CLOSER to success?

_____
_____
_____
_____
_____
_____
_____
_____
_____
_____
_____
_____
_____
_____
_____
_____

Genie Craff

CHALLENGE 71: Vision
*"Keep your face to the sunshine and
you can never see the shadow."
~~Helen Keller*

PROFITS Affirmation: I keep my face to the SUNSHINE.

POWER Word: SUNSHINE

My Affirmation:
_____
_____

Profitable Trading Wisdom: Describe how a great FOREX trade for you allows you to keep your face to the SUNSHINE.

_____
_____
_____
_____
_____
_____
_____
_____
_____
_____
_____
_____
_____
_____
_____
_____
_____

CHALLENGE 72: Vision
"The moment you are old enough to take the wheel,
Responsibility lies with you."
~~J. K. Rowling

PROFITS Affirmation: I am in control of my emotions MOMENT by MOMENT.

POWER Word: MOMENT

My Affirmation:
_____
_____

Profitable Trading Wisdom: Explain how every MOMENT is a fresh beginning when you trade FOREX.

_____
_____
_____
_____
_____
_____
_____
_____
_____
_____
_____
_____
_____
_____
_____
_____
_____

CHALLENGE 73: SUCCESS

"A mediocre idea that generates enthusiasm will go further than a great idea which inspires no one."
~~Mary Kay Ash

PROFITS Affirmation: I have ideas which generate my ENTHUSIASM.

POWER Word: ENTHUSIASM

My Affirmation:
_____
_____

Profitable Trading Wisdom: A mediocre idea of mine which generates ENTHUSIAM for me is:

CHALLENGE 74: Success
"The successful warrior is the average (wo)man with laser-like focus."
~~Bruce Lee

PROFITS Affirmation: I have laser-like FOCUS

POWER Word: FOCUS

My Affirmation:
___

Profitable Trading Wisdom: My laser-like FOCUS keeps me on track when I am feeling…

CHALLENGE 75: Success

*"Success is not only about what you
accomplish in your life;
it's about what you inspire others to do."*
~~Unknown

PROFITS Affirmation: I am successful when I ACCOMPLISH what I want to.

POWER Word: ACCOMPLISH

My Affirmation:
_____
_____

Profitable Trading Wisdom: My success is multiplied when I ACCOMPLISH what I want to. I ACCOMPLISH these 5 THINGS.

_____
_____
_____
_____
_____
_____
_____
_____
_____
_____
_____
_____
_____
_____
_____

CHALLENGE 76: Success
"There are no secrets to success.
It is the result of preparation,
hard work and learning from failure"
~~Colin Powell

PROFITS Affirmation: I embrace the knowledge that there are no SECRETS to success.

POWER Word: SECRETS

My Affirmation:
_____
_____

Profitable Trading Wisdom: What are your SECRETS of preparation, working hard, and learning from failure?

CHALLENGE 77: Success

*"The real test is not that you avoid this failure, because you won't.
It is whether you let it harden or
shame you into inaction,
or whether you learn from it or
whether you choose to persevere."*
~~President Barak Obama, 44th President of the U.S.

PROFITS Affirmation: I PERSERVERE through FOREX trading failures.

POWER Word: PERSERVERE

My Affirmation:
___

Profitable Trading Wisdom: I do the following 4 things to PERSERVERE through FOREX trading failure.
___

CHALLENGE 78: BIG Dreams
"Everything you want is just
outside of your comfort zone."
~~Robert Allen

PROFITS Affirmation: Today, I know everything I want is just OUTSIDE my comfort zone!

POWER Word: OUTSIDE

My Affirmation:
_____
_____

Profitable Trading Wisdom: Describe how everything you want is OUTSIDE of your comfort zone.

_____
_____
_____
_____
_____
_____
_____
_____
_____
_____
_____
_____
_____
_____
_____

CHALLENGE 79: BIG Dreams
"I learned that being around
another dreamer can
push you when you forget
how to dream for yourself."
~~Steve Harvey, Act Like A Success, p. 147

PROFITS Affirmation: I spend time with another DREAMER.

POWER Word: DREAMER

My Affirmation:
_____
_____

Profitable Trading Wisdom: Share a little about the other DREAMER you spend time with.

_____
_____
_____
_____
_____
_____
_____
_____
_____
_____
_____
_____

CHALLENGE 80: BIG Dreams
"The journey of a thousand miles
must begin with a small step."
~~Chinese Proverb

PROFITS Affirmation: I began my FOREX JOURNEY with a small step.

POWER Word: JOURNEY

My Affirmation:
_____
_____

Profitable Trading Wisdom: Looking back, what small step started your FOREX JOURNEY?

Genie Craff

CHALLENGE 81: BIG Dreams
*"The future belongs to those who believe
in the beauty of their dreams."
~~Eleanor Roosevelt*

PROFITS Affirmation: There is BEAUTY in my BIG Dreams.

POWER Word: BEAUTY

My Affirmation:
_____
_____

Profitable Trading Wisdom: Paint a verbal picture of the BEAUTY in your new FOREX trading BIG Dreams!

_____
_____
_____
_____
_____
_____
_____
_____
_____
_____
_____
_____
_____
_____
_____
_____
_____

CHALLENGE 82: BIG Dreams
*"I believe every human has
a finite number of heartbeats.
I don't intend to waste any of mine."
~~Neil Armstrong*

PROFITS Affirmation: I use every one of my HEARTBEATS to live my life to the fullest!

POWER Word: HEARTBEATS

My Affirmation:
_____
_____

Profitable Trading Wisdom: Use a few HEARTBEATS to describe what has changed the most since you started your FOREX journey?

_____
_____
_____
_____
_____
_____
_____
_____
_____
_____
_____
_____
_____
_____
_____

CHAPTER 12: ABUNDANT GRATITUDE LIFESTYLE

"Acknowledging the good that you already have in your life is the foundation for all ABUNDANCE."
~~Eckart Tolle

Short Story: I have a very awesome friend. We share a similar success vision. I am fortunate enough to live in her favorite city. She comes to visit more when the sun shines less in the mountains. She loves the sun! I was very excited to discover she would be in town. We had arranged to go to the mall together to chat, to catch up and have a yummy lunch.

After lunch, we practiced guiltless shopping. We tried on fashions that two years ago we would not have thought of even looking at. We shopped in stores where they have a specialist for every individual brand of clothing and for some of the most VIP customers a personal fashion consultant. No clothes were on the shiny tiled floors of these shops! What a wonderful experience.

I have learned many things from her. She has taught me how to study FOREX for anywhere from 2 to 4 hours a day. She excellently shares what she has learned about trading in the most casual of ways, sometimes with perfect strangers and sometimes with the most experienced traders. She described how she leads her interested parties through a very simple introduction to Mindset Mastery. Supporting gently when needed and providing direct instruction when necessary. Her trading journey, just like the rest of her lifestyle, used to be her vision. That vision is now her dream.

"Cultivate the habit of being grateful for every good thing that comes to you..."
~Ralph Waldo Emerson

I had the honor to take her back to the airport a couple of days later, but in the meantime, we shared stories of the incredible people we met along our separate trading journeys. Yes, not all have joined our trading journey. She has taught me to look for only those who are serious about having, Mindset Mastery, commas in their bank account balance, and a desire to live the life of their dreams. I thank her for sharing her time, her integrity, her voice, her wisdom and her expertise. Her friendship is an unexpected blessing. Most would not recognize her on the street, but then, that is not what she would be expecting.

An old plaque hung on a wall in a classroom. The message is still relevant today.

>The six most important words:
>I admit that I was wrong.
>The five most important words:
>You did a great job!
>The four most important words:
>What do you think?
>The three most important words:
>Could you please…
>The two most important words.
>Thank YOU.
>The most important word:
>WE.
>The least important word:
>I.

---

*"Our children are our living messengers
to a future we will never see."
~~United States Representative, Elijah Cummings*

When you have the ultimate "say so", you will live the life of your visions, success and dreams differently. Learn what you can about how wealth can deliver all you want in your life and for those you love. Be among those looking for places for wealth to grow. Share with others what you learn about finances and wealth.

Find ways to share your wealth, from your personal beliefs. Give back. Some may find themselves already giving to those less fortunate. Others may be volunteering with a cause they love. They share their Gratitude every time they volunteer.

Volunteering provides a new level of self-awareness and consistent confidence. The simplest most meaningful blessings are those received after Gratitude has been shared.

---

*"The great courageous act that we all must do is to have the COURAGE to step out
of our history and past,
So that we can live our DREAM."
~~Oprah Winfrey*

CHALLENGE 83: The Abundant GRATITUDE Lifestyle
"As you grow older, you will discover that
you have two hands,
one for helping yourself, the other
for helping others."
~~Audrey Hepburn

PROFITS Affirmation: My Gratitude for HELPING others helps me help myself.

POWER Word: HELPING

My Affirmation:
_____
_____

Profitable Trading Wisdom: Describe how grateful you feel when you are HELPING others.

_____
_____
_____
_____
_____
_____
_____
_____
_____
_____
_____
_____
_____
_____

CHALLENGE 84: The Abundant GRATITUDE Lifestyle
"Well done is better than well said."
~~Benjamin Franklin

PROFITS Affirmation: Every Evening, I can say "WELL DONE" because I did _____ all day long.

POWER Word: WELL DONE

My Affirmation:

_____
_____

Profitable Trading Wisdom: Describe 2 things on your "WELL DONE" list today.

_____
_____
_____
_____
_____
_____
_____
_____
_____
_____
_____
_____
_____
_____
_____
_____
_____
_____
_____

CHALLENGE 85: The Abundant GRATITUDE Lifestyle
*"It is in giving that I connect with others,
with the world and with the Devine."*
~~Isabelle Allende

PROFITS Affirmation: I love GIVING to others regularly.

POWER Word: GIVING

My Affirmation:
_____
_____

Profitable Trading Wisdom: List 3 people who have benefited from your personal GIVING.

CHALLENGE 86: The Abundant GRATITUDE Lifestyle

*"If you get the inside right,
the outside will fall into place."*
~~Eckard Tolle

PROFITS Affirmation: Today, My INSIDE is right!

POWER Word: INSDIDE

My Affirmation:
___

Profitable Trading Wisdom: List 4 ways your INSIDE has been made right.

CHALLENGE 87: The Abundant GRATITUDE Lifestyle

"The more you praise and celebrate your life,
the more there is in life to celebrate."
~~Oprah Winfrey

PROFITS Affirmation: I praise and CELEBRATE everything in my life!

POWER Word: CELEBRATE

My Affirmation:
_____
_____

Profitable Trading Wisdom: List 5 things you CELEBRATE today.

CHAPTER 13: CHALLENGE COMPLETION LOG

"Think of yourself as on the threshold of unparalleled success.
A whole, clear, glorious life lies before you.
Achieve! Achieve!
~~Andrew Carnegie

--CHALLENGE COMPLETION LOG--

Mindset Mastery skills build your personal belief into consistent confidence allowing you to develop FOREX trading skills. Vision and success deliver the lifestyle of your dreams in Abundant Gratitude. Complete the following POWER WORD Challenges as you need them, enter the date you complete each one.

Chapter 1 - Mindset Mastery for Belief & Consistent Confidence
Challenge #1. Date: _____ CHOICES - Messages Growing Up
Challenge #2. Date: _____ LIMITATIONS - Hold Me Back
Challenge #3. Date: _____ ASTOUND - Astound Me
Challenge #4. Date: _____ HABIT - Positive Habits
Challenge #5. Date: _____ BELIEVE - Believe in Me

Chapter 2 - Focus on WHY
Challenge #6. Date: _____ DECIDED - What I Want
Challenge #7. Date: _____ INNOVATIVE - Greater Innovation
Challenge #8. Date: _____ PURPOSE - Impact My Purpose
Challenge #9. Date: _____ TRUST - Partners Appear
Challenge #10. Date: _____ FOUND - Found WHY
Challenge #11. Date: _____ AIM - Highest Aim
Challenge #12. Date: _____ FEEDBACK - Behavior & Opportunity
Challenge #13. Date: _____ FORGIVE - Forgive Yourself
Challenge #14. Date: _____ DOING - What Others Won't
Challenge #15. Date: _____ CREATE - Positive Future S

Pip$ Profit$ & Power

Chapter 3 – Mindset Mastery Elements, Mentoring & Taking Responsibility
Challenge #16. Date: _____ RESPONSIBILE – Finances, Wealth &n Prosperity
Challenge #17. Date: _____ COMMAND – My Thoughts
Challenge #18. Date: _____ STARTED – Now What?
Challenge #19. Date: _____ MIND – Rise Above Misfortune
Challenge #20. Date: _____ GREATNESS – Pay the Price

Chapter 4 – Grounded Trading Goals
Challenge #21. Date: _____ INVENT – My Future
Challenge #22. Date: _____ ACT – To Become
Challenge #23. Date: _____ BEGIN – 10-year Goals
Challenge #24. Date: _____ SERIOUS – Almost Goals
Challenge #25. Date: _____ SIMPLE – Life is Simple

Chapter 5 – Prosperity Trading Plan
Challenge #26. Date: _____ WORKS – What Works for Me
Challenge #27. Date: _____ LEADING – Leading Me
Challenge #28. Date: _____ PRACTICE – DEMO Practice
Challenge #29. Date: _____ EFFORTS – Small Efforts
Challenge #30. Date: _____ IMPORTANT – Planning IS Important

Chapter 6 – Unbreakable Trading Rules
Challenge #31. Date: _____ WORK – Work on Rules
Challenge #32. Date: _____ RULES – Rules Assist
Challenge #33. Date: _____ EXCEPTIONS – No Exceptions
Challenge #34. Date: _____ CARE – Show Others You Care
Challenge #35. Date: _____ MASTERED – Mastered Rules

Chapter 7 – Trade Entry Indicators
Challenge #36. Date: _____ PRINCIPLE – Principled Decisions
Challenge #37. Date: _____ VICTORY – Tools Needed
Challenge #38. Date: _____ INTENTION – Intention Signals
Challenge #39. Date: _____ EXPECTATIONS – Formed Expectations
Challenge #40. Date: _____ TOOLS – Towards Victory

Chapter 8 – Incorporating Daily Education/Learning
Challenge #41. Date: _____ LEARNING – Education + Learning = Leadership
Challenge #42. Date: _____ RESISTANCE – "Stand-out" Education/Training
Challenge #43. Date: _____ PLAY – Rules to Enter and Exit Trades

Challenge #44. Date: _____ NEEDS – Active Listening
Challenge #45. Date: _____ COUNTS – I Learned

Chapter 9 – Passion & GREED
Challenge #46. Date: _____ STRENGTH – New Day Brings
Challenge #47. Date: _____ PASSIONATE – Passionate FOREX Trading
Challenge #48. Date: _____ SETTLING – So Worth Living
Challenge #49. Date: _____ REASON – Reason Holds the Reigns
Challenge #50. Date: _____ LIFE – A Passionate Life
Challenge #51. Date: _____ LISTENED – Great Advice
Challenge #52. Date: _____ SLIPPED – Proper FOREX
Challenge #53. Date: _____ WRONG – Emotions Contained
Challenge #54. Date: _____ EXPERIENCE – Experience Can Be Expensive
Challenge #55. Date: _____ ANXIETY – Protecting the $$$$$ in my Account

Chapter 10 – Responsible Risk Management
Challenge #56. Date: _____ SUCCESS – Failed Over and Over
Challenge #57. Date: _____ IGNORANCE – Ignorance Cost Me
Challenge #58. Date: _____ MEASURE – Better Person
Challenge #59. Date: _____ CHASING – Chasing My Dream
Challenge #60. Date: _____ FACED – I Faced…

Chapter 11 – WOMEN in FOREX (For Your Eyes Only)
Challenge #61. Date: _____ BELIEVED – She Believed…
Challenge #62. Date: _____ INTEGRITY – Integrity Motivates
Challenge #63. Date: _____ POWER– Power All Along
Challenge #64. Date: _____ COURAGE – Like A Muscle
Challenge #65. Date: _____ PEACE – Controls Emotions
Challenge #66. Date: _____ CHARISMATIC – When I Trade FOREX
Challenge #67. Date: _____ INSPIRE – Inspire Me

Chapter 12 – Vision, Success & Dream BIG
Challenge #68. Date: _____ AGAIN – Succeed Again
Challenge #69. Date: _____ IMAGINATION – Preview Coming Attractions
Challenge #70. Date: _____ CLOSER– Closer to Success
Challenge #71. Date: _____ SUNSHINE – Face to the Sunshine
Challenge #72. Date: _____ MOMENT – Fresh Beginning
Challenge #73. Date: _____ ENTHUSIASM – High Enthusiasm
Challenge #74. Date: _____ FOCUS – Laser-like Focus

Challenge #75. Date: _____ ACCOMPLISH – I Accomplish…

Chapter 13 – Abundant GRATITUDE
Challenge #76. Date: _____ SECRETS – Secrets of Success
Challenge #77. Date: _____ PERSERVERANCE – Through Trading Failure
Challenge #78. Date: _____ OUTSIDE – Outside My Comfort Zone
Challenge #79. Date: _____ DREAMER – The Other Dreamer
Challenge #80. Date: _____ JOURNEY – My Small Step
Challenge #81. Date: _____ BEAUTY – Beauty in FOREX
Challenge #82. Date: _____ HEARTBEATS – Most Changed
Challenge #83. Date: _____ HELPING – Helping Others
Challenge #84. Date: _____ WELL DONE – Well Done List
Challenge #85. Date: _____ GIVING – Personal Giving
Challenge #86. Date: _____ INSIDE – Inside Made Right
Challenge #87. Date: _____ CELEBRATE, CELEBRATE TODAY

CONCLUSION

TRADER'S THEME SONG

"You gotta know when the trend is up,
know when the trend is down,
know the best lot size,
know when to take your profit.
You nev'r count your money
when you're at the trading table,
there'll be time enough for countin'
when the tradin's done."
--Adapted Song by Kenny Rogers